Denise Parker
A Teenage Archer's Quest for Olympic Glory

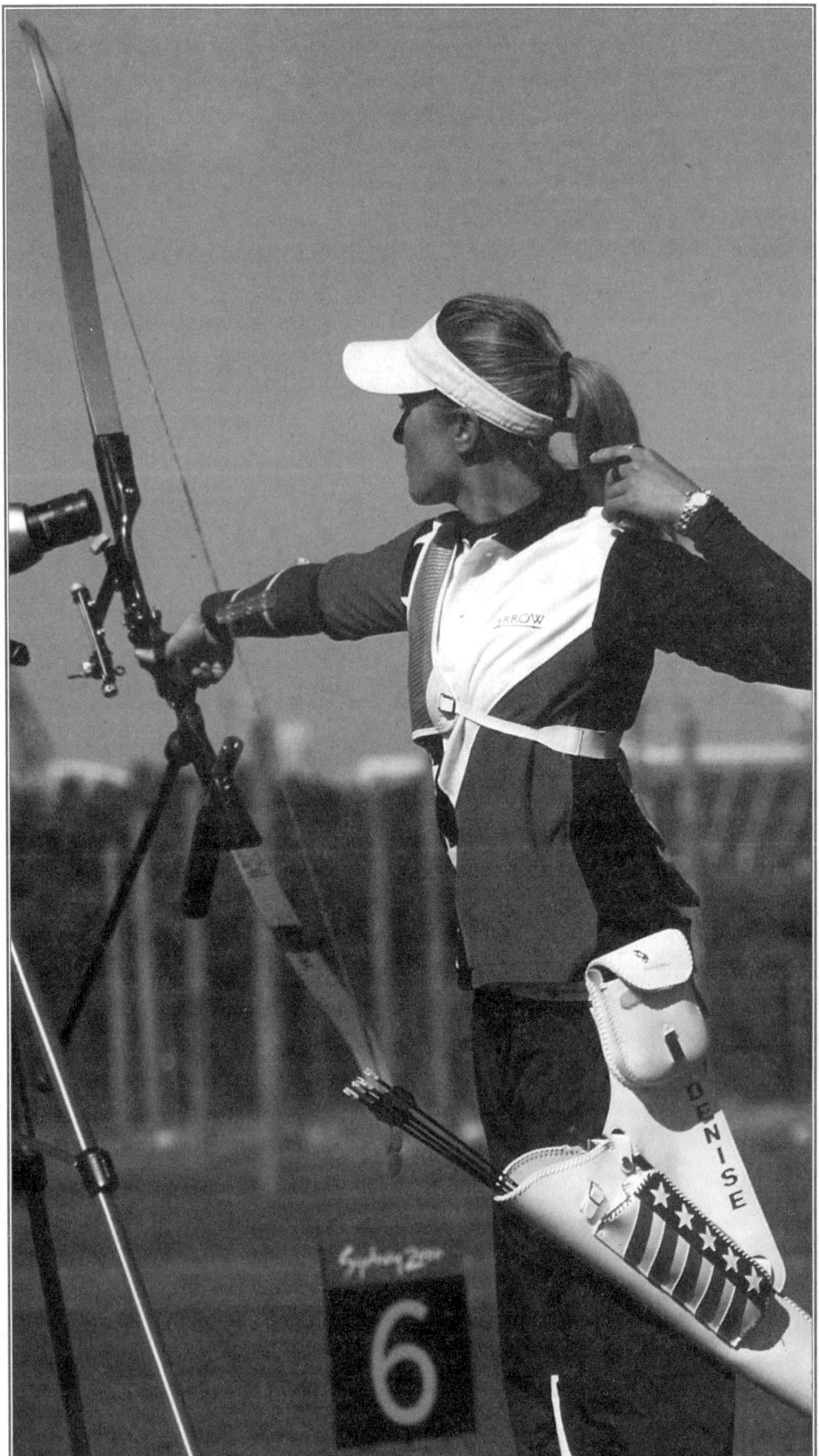
DENISE
6

ArrowSport

Denise Parker
A Teenage Archer's Quest for Olympic Glory

**Denise Parker
with Kathy Etling**

© Woods N' Water Press
P.O. Box 550, Florida, New York 10921
All Rights Reserved

To my children Jake and Nicklaus,
and step daughters, Madeline and McCayla

"May you always find inspiration and never be bound by expectation."

Through the process of working on this book I realized how important it is for children to have a focus in life with their own goals and passions to drive them in a positive direction on a daily basis. Without a target and path, they can so easily stray. As parents our goal is to try to help them find their own passions and support and encourage them in this process. I hope very much that both children and parents alike find this book to be helpful in their own process of discovery as smooth or tumultuous as it may be. I want to thank ArrowSport and the Archery Trade Association for helping bring this book to fruition and what a wonderful thing to be able to give back to the sport that has given me so much. Proceeds from this book will help others find opportunities to participate in archery. For that, I am proud to be a part of the program.

Denise Parker

Denise Parker's rise to international fame as an archer was largely due to her parents and to her love for archery. Today, Denise's story is a realistic possibility for thousands of school-age boys and girls in nearly every state because of the National Archery in the Schools Program (NASP). For years, archery has been a backyard, informal sport—that is until the NASP began in Kentucky in 2002. NASP has introduced archery to kids as part of their Physical Education curriculum during the school day. Young girls have become especially good at shooting bows and arrows which means many have a chance to realize an Olympic dream. The proceeds from this book will add to the $600,000 ATA has already spent to fund school and community archery programs. Your purchase will ensure that future archers who aspire to follow Denise Parker will get their chance.

Jay McAninch, CEO/President, Archery Trade Association

Brief quotations may be used in article reviews. For any other reproduction of the book including electronic, mechanical, photographic, recording, CD-ROM, videotaping, laser or computer disc, or other means, written permission must first be obtained from the publisher Woods N' Water, Inc.

Front and back photos courtesy of Denise Parker. All interior photos by the author unless noted otherwise.

Published by Woods N' Water, Inc., P.O. Box 550, 468 Route 17A, 2nd Fl., Florida, NY 10921. Our toll-free number for orders is 800-652-7527. Our web site is www.atabooks.com. All other inquiries about this and other ArrowSport titles, may call 845-986-0326.

Printed in the United States of America

10 9 8 7 6 5 4 3 2 1

ISBN-13: 978-0-9795131-1-4
ISBN-10: 0-9795131-1-1

Table of Contents

Preface vi

Chapter 1 – An Ordinary Girl 1

Chapter 2 – An Unusual Talent: Archery–What's That? 15

Chapter 3 – I Have Potential! 25

Chapter 4 – My First Competition 31

Chapter 5 – Winning! 35

Chapter 6 – Dealing with Pressure 53

Chapter 7 – Qualifying for the Olympics 69

Chapter 8 – The Olympic Atmosphere 87

Chapter 9 – A Place in the Sun — and on the Podium 103

Chapter 10 – Struggling Under Expectations 115

Chapter 11 – The Meltdown 133

Chapter 12 – The Comeback 147

Chapter 13 – Life: So Much More! 161

Preface
Why You Should Read This Book

As I write these words, nearly seven years have passed since I was part of the United States' Olympic archery team. Even with so much time to reflect, I sometimes struggle to comprehend — and share — much of what I learned during my 13 years on archery's world stage.

Maybe that's because although I was 26 during the 2000 Games in Sydney, Australia, those were already my third Olympics. And except for a poor outing late in the 1996 trials, Sydney would have been my fourth Olympics. In other words, my pursuit of the Olympics and the excitement of competing in the Games dominated half of my first 26 years.

I was 14 and already living a girlhood dream at the 1988 Olympics in Seoul, South Korea, where I helped the U.S. women win a bronze medal in the team competition. In many ways I was too young to fully appreciate that accomplishment, and I most certainly wasn't prepared for the road ahead.

Soon after Seoul, I was no longer considered a child prodigy. As people's expectations of me changed, I had to sprint emotionally to keep up with the complex adult world in which I was living. I was constantly surprised by the depth and breadth of people's strengths and frailties. By age 18 at the 1992 Games in Barcelona, I was realizing how much my naïveté at Seoul had shielded me from various pressures and personalities. No longer could I simply classify people as "nice" or "mean."

As I left my teen years behind, I also learned age, experience and practice didn't improve my every shortcoming. I finally realized I couldn't control everything swirling through my life. By age 22, I was in full panic while trying to make the 1996 Olympic team. There I was a young woman, but I often wished I could again be like my fearless 13-year-old self who won gold at the 1987 Pan Am Games. Life and archery had been so free of complications back then!

Lacking my previous focus and confidence, I knew I couldn't make the Olympics at Atlanta in 1996, and I didn't. That failure, however, helped motivate me for the 2000 Olympics in Sydney. I wouldn't let that disappointment define me as an Olympic archer. I recommitted myself to this sport, regained my confidence, and then reclaimed my spot on Team USA. Although I didn't do as well as I hoped at the 2000 Games, I returned home content. I moved on with satisfaction, not regret, and focused my competitive energies into my career.

True, I never again enjoyed the success I experienced at age 14 in archery, but I realized something equally important: Once you've repeatedly pushed

Preface

yourself as far as your natural talents allow, you're entitled to take pride in your accomplishments. You can't let others determine your expectations and control your happiness. After all, most people can't know your capabilities, and they certainly can't judge what your goals should be.

Perhaps that is why I wanted to share my story with you. Mine isn't a fairy tale that ends with Olympic gold. My story is about the value of realizing your individual gifts, recognizing the talents of others, and appreciating the help you receive from family, friends and supporters.

I believe everyone can inspire and be inspired, but personally, I don't have individual idols in sports or elsewhere. Maybe that's because I've met many talented, helpful, self-motivated people, and few of them have won a gold medal or championship ring. In fact, for every gold-medalist on an Olympic podium, there's a thousand more people around the world who worked equally hard to maximize their talents but still fell short.

That doesn't mean an event has one winner and a thousand losers. It means at least a thousand skilled people deserve our praise, and we can learn from them. It's even possible they have more to teach us than the victors themselves. As the poet Emily Dickinson wrote:

> *"Success is counted sweetest*
> *By those who ne'er succeed.*
> *To comprehend a nectar*
> *Requires sorest need."*

I still cry at the end of some sporting events, because I know how hard every athlete worked to get there. Each one of them struggled at some point, but by setting high goals and striving to reach them, they improved themselves and those who surround them.

I think that's the true value of competition, whether it's in high school, college, recreational leagues, professional sports or the workplace. Competition and hard work are enriching, rewarding values, as long as we keep them in balance.

But if we become obsessed with winning or living up to others' expectations, or letting another person's performance determine our own happiness, we will never find fulfillment or satisfaction. We'll get nothing but frustration, because the harder people try to overcome an unhealthy obsession, the less fun they have and the less consistently they perform.

I also hope coaches and parents will read my story and learn from it. It's important to provide children a variety of opportunities in sports and

Preface

academics. With luck they'll discover their natural talents. Offer them advice and encouragement, but step back if you find your mood changes based on their performance. If they start using your mood to determine their own, you're both bound for disappointments.

Realize, too, that even if we let stress and pressure affect our work and play, we can start over the next day. Opportunities often arise from setbacks, and even from tragedies. For example, my biological father died before I ever knew him. My mother persevered and eventually remarried.

I often wish I could somehow sit down and talk to my biological father, but I also realize if it weren't for my stepfather I probably never would have become an Olympic archer. As you'll read, we eventually had to sever the coach/athlete relationship to preserve the more important father/daughter relationship, but I know he sacrificed incredible amounts of time, energy and money to help me reach my Olympic dreams.

Of course, I'll never know what I missed by losing my biological father so young, but I do know what I gained because of my stepfather. Maybe that's why I would never cash in my stack of chips just to see what was behind Door Number 2.

And now, as I sit here wondering what lies ahead for my own children, I can only hope we create many great memories of our own in the years to come.

— Denise Parker, May 2007

Chapter 1
An Ordinary Girl

The Early Years

Denise Parker, the youngest Olympic archery medalist the United States has ever produced, remembers very little from when she was quite young. Or perhaps she's just chosen to forget much of what transpired during her earliest years.

Denise, then known as Denise Knudson, was a toddler of three when her biological father died of cancer. Having her father die affected the youngster, but not as much as the man's loss affected Denise's mother, Valerie.

Valerie was no stranger to emotional turmoil. Losing her husband Knudson was but the latest tragedy in the woman's life. Valerie's father—Denise's grandfather—Douglas Vowles, was an engineer by profession who was told by doctors that they'd discovered a tumor growing on his spine. At the time, little could be done surgically to help patients suffering from such debilitating diseases of the central nervous system, which includes the nerve-rich spinal cord. Valerie watched her father struggle with an enemy he had no chance of beating, and yet the man never gave up. Mr. Vowles, who was paralyzed from the neck down, continued to support his family by selling insurance over a special phone, modified to operate from the motion of his mouth.

When Denise later displayed the same tenacity and resolve during international competitions, Valerie Knudson wasn't surprised. The very traits that helped the girl achieve so much, in such a short period of time, had to be recognizable to the woman as identical to those that kept Valerie's own father determined to provide for his family well after other men would have given up.

After Mr. Knudson's death, Valerie found a job as a secretary. The position didn't pay much, and one of Denise's earliest memories during this time was the difficulty the pair confronted as they tried to survive on her mother's salary alone.

Denise's two half-brothers were living with their father part-time or the little family might not have made it financially. The boys, 10 and 11 years older than Denise, were too much older than their baby sister to figure very prominently in her life.

Finding Father

When Denise was five, Valerie met and fell in love with Earl Parker, a printer for The Newspaper Agency, publishers of Salt Lake City's two daily newspapers. "Earl is the only father I've ever really known," explained Denise. Earl Parker made a huge difference in both Knudsons' lives. Everything seemed to change for the better, including the future which now appeared much brighter.

Earl Parker, born and raised in the hardscrabble hills of West Virginia's coal-mining country, was as familiar with hardship as the Knudsons. After he'd graduated from high school he'd enlisted in the Air Force for three years. He learned the printing trade and, although always able to find work, the man's restless streak kept him on the move. Earl had the wanderlust, and yet he had no idea why.

When Earl set eyes on Utah, his restlessness eased its grip on him. The man felt an immediate kinship with the state's soaring mountains and vast sagebrush prairies. He then met Valerie Knudson, and the puzzle pieces comprising the three separate lives meshed to create one loving unit. Earl, Valerie and Denise came together and each realized that all suddenly was right in their world.

Valerie Knudson married Earl and changed her last name to his. Denise, suddenly conscious of possessing a last name different from theirs, asked if she too might become a Parker. The request touched Earl deeply. In the months and years to come the pair would come to share an incredible father-daughter relationship, one closer than that enjoyed by most fathers and their biological offspring.

Earl Parker was well-suited to be the father of Valerie's daring, inquisitive 5-year-old. Parker, like Denise, brimmed with enthusiasm for life and its wonders. He loved being outside in nature, and was an avid trout angler, hunter, golfer, runner and motorcyclist. One of Earl's finest traits was to see possibility in almost anything, and as Denise came to share her father's desire for living and adventure, his indomitable spirit affected her in a positive manner as well.

Not that she needed any help. Denise had already revealed a natural affinity for sport—any sport. If the other kids were outside playing a game, Denise wanted to join them. If Earl tried a new outdoors activity, Denise would wait nearby for the chance to share in the fun, as soon as her Dad would permit it.

Valerie, through her new husband, had also discovered she loved the outdoors. Before long, the entire family was inseparable thanks to their enjoyment of each other and their common interests. If one Parker was seen having fun, the other two were either similarly engaged nearby or getting ready to join the party.

Not until the Parkers finally settled down in the little town of South Jordan, then a rural suburb of Salt Lake City, did the Parkers truly put down roots. Denise remembers their South Jordan home with fondness because it had been built in a development surrounded

My father teaching me how to ride my motorcycle.

by open spaces where she roamed and explored, played sports and rode her dirt bike.

The house served as the Parkers' operational base during the work and school week. The recreational vehicle, or RV, they purchased next became central to the family's weekend and vacation fun. Visitors would find the Parker house by looking for the RV in the driveway, an RV that soon became one of the family's greatest pleasures. Whenever they could they'd pack up gear and provisions, then Mr. Parker would climb up into the fully-loaded RV's cab, start the engine and nose the vehicle into the mountains where the family would camp, hike, search for arrowheads, fish or hunt.

Traditional little girl pastimes like playing with dolls never piqued Denise's interest. Sports were what intrigued her, mainly football, basketball, soccer and catch. "No matter what the weather, we'd be outside playing," she said. "One of my first memories is of playing winter basketball in our neighbor's yard. That day was bitterly cold. My hands felt like they were frozen. I hurried back inside to thaw them out beneath the hot water faucet, and then rushed back outside as quickly as possible so I wouldn't miss a minute more playing time than necessary."

A Special Closeness

Earl Parker, unlike many stepfathers, treated Denise like his own blood kin. In return, Denise considered Earl her real father. The two grew closer until Denise truly was Earl Parker's daughter in every way but biological, and that mattered nothing to either of them. "My father became my life's driving force," Denise recalled. "He taught me to love hunting, fishing, motorbikes, running and golf. Even better was the fun we had whenever the two of us were together."

Earl bought the young tomboy a single golf club, a 3-iron, when she was seven. "When I go to the practice tee, you bring your 3-iron," instructed Earl. "If you ever get to a point where you can drive a golf ball a hundred yards with your club, I'll buy you a complete set of golf clubs."

The challenge had been issued, and the youngster soon could whack a golf ball a hundred yards. Denise had come through, and now her father did as well: she soon owned the coveted set of clubs.

"My Dad loved riding motorcycles, so he bought one for my Mom and a dirt bike for me," said Denise. "I was only seven at the time, but how I loved to race my bike and go off the jumps on the track we'd built in the field behind our house."

I loved playing all types of sports. Here I am playing in an All-Star softball game.

Would it ever be possible, Valerie Parker wondered, to mold the little daredevil into a proper young lady?

"My mother has always been a very elegant woman," explained Denise. "She tried to interest me in ballet through dance classes, but I thought ballet was awful. She signed me up for piano lessons, but I hated them. I was only interested in going outside and playing. Mom would complain, 'How did I get a daughter interested only in sports?'

"I always did well in school," she continued. "I loved math, and I won a Reflections Essay Contest when I was in second grade." Denise explained that the win was especially meaningful since all the kids in her elementary school were eligible to compete in the contest. "The title of my winning essay was *What Makes Me Smile*," said Denise. "I used my essay to explain how wonderful I would feel whenever I made a goal while playing soccer."

A Teenage Archer's Quest for Olympic Glory

Reading Denise's winning essay made Valerie finally understand how important sports and competition, even if only for fun, were to her daughter. "If that's what makes Denise happy, why am I bothering her with music and ballet?" her mother wondered.

And that is how studies and sports came to consume the greatest part of Denise Parker's young life.

I would be like a "pit crew" for a my dad during his motorcycle races.

7

Nobody's Fool

One thing that has always made Denise Parker stand out from a crowd was her decision, at an early age, always to be an individual.

"I've always had a mind of my own and not easily swayed. I've always tried to stay focused on whatever I was doing and do it to the best of my ability," Denise said.

Giving her all, no matter what, endeared her to her teammates, most of whom were boys. The boys with whom Denise was chummy didn't think it odd that a girl was one of their gang. They knew she was a tough competitor, and that's what mattered most, which is probably why Denise's best friends, when she was in elementary and middle school were boys.

Denise bailed out on the boys, but just once—when they decided to use firecrackers to blow up grasshoppers.

A Different Time

Denise's childhood and teenaged years scrolled by during a time when girls' athletics received little attention or funding from school sports departments. Boys' sports programs and team activities received the greater majority—if not the entire budget—allocated to sports in co-educational schools.

It took a landmark decision, later known as Title IX, handed down by the U. S. Supreme Court before all schools and universities that received federal tax dollars were required, by law, to spend equitably on male and female sports programs alike. Title IX marked the beginning of a new era in girls' and women's sports, an era during which many Americans have grown to adulthood without being fully aware of the extent of the unfairness that once existed in girls' sports.

Funding may have been tight for girls' sports in the schools Denise attended, but the entire Parker family never wavered in their enthusiasm for the youngster's participation in athletics. Earl Parker, in particular, did whatever was humanly possible to help his daughter excel in whatever sport she was involved in at the moment.

Daddy's Girl

Each morning, Earl Parker's newspaper job required him to rise early and leave for work soon afterwards. Parker's early starting time at work meant he'd be back at home no later than 3:00 or 3:30 p.m. each afternoon. His work schedule provided the man with an abundance of free time and he chose to spend most of it with his daughter.

"I became Dad's best buddy," recalled Denise. "I look back on that time and I really appreciate the many sacrifices he made for me" (that weren't always apparent to me at the time).

Mr. Parker was a firm believer in the value of practice as a means to reach a goal, and did his best to instill a similar belief in his daughter.

"I enjoyed playing league basketball, but I wasn't a very (accomplished) dribbler," said Denise. "Dad set up a series of cones in the basement and challenged me to practice dribbling the ball, without losing it, through them. When I could do it consistently, he said he'd buy me a cat."

Motivated by both the desire for the cat and to do well made Denise concentrate on the task at hand. She practiced diligently and that cat soon was hers. With each challenge surmounted, Denise gained a great appreciation of practice's value in attaining a desired goal.

A Competitive Fire

The more the youngster accomplished, the more she wanted to do, and do well. Succeeding at smaller goals made the girl more determined to achieve larger ones. She lived for and thrived on challenges.

Being a mere spectator was never enough for the girl. The thick of the action was where she wanted, needed to be; competing even if it was possible. And if it weren't possible, well, she would find a way to make it possible. That's just the way she was made.

Why she was wired like she was, she had no idea. Sometimes, however, she'd reflect on why some people are driven so furiously to compete, like she was, while others seemed perfectly content observing from afar.

That within this slight youngster raged a competitive fire became evident one brilliant day at a cross-country youth race. The entire Parker family enjoyed cross-country racing, perhaps spurred on by the knowledge that Earl Parker had completed two 26-mile marathons. On this occasion, Denise seemed to have the race well in hand when one of her running shoes flew completely off her foot as she continued to speed along the course.

Stop? Not on your life. She simply continued to run full out until she'd crossed the finish line still in first place.

Did her father, the marathoner, serve as inspiration? Perhaps, to some extent. But when someone later inquired as to why she'd kept running without her shoe, Denise simply said, "I was afraid the kid behind me would catch up."

Having that kid catch her would have ranked as a huge tragedy in young Parker's mind. Even today, when asked to sum up her childhood years, her answer explains rather precisely who she was and who she would become. "I wanted to win," she said.

Growing Confidence

Win the youngster did. And with each small victory Denise's confidence increased. The more she won or succeeded, the more convinced she became that perhaps she really **could** do anything. No all girls' teams? She and girlfriend, Kaprice Gunn, simply played soccer and basketball with the boys.

Denise admitted that she'll still occasionally flip through journal entries made during her youth and recall how she felt at the moment they were written. "Remembering a goal I scored or another way I may have helped my team to victory helps me relive the moment," she said.

The confidence she was gaining was of crucial importance, as was the immense satisfaction that came from winning. More integral to her happiness, however, was the knowledge that her parents were totally behind her in everything she did. Like all youngsters, with no conception of what might lie ahead, Denise was sometimes prone to

My friend Kaprice and me at a local running race.

make bold pronouncements or announce grand plans. She was young. She really did believe there was nothing she could not do were she to put her mind to it. And yet the Parkers wisely never laughed or made fun of their daughter. "My parents were there for me, no matter what I tried next," said Denise. "They reinforced my belief that I **could** do anything if I focused intently on my goal and worked hard."

True Grit

Westerners are fond of those who try their best and refuse to give up. Such people, they'll say, have 'sand,' 'grit' or 'bottom.' Those words imply that the individual will always find something extra to keep her going. Denise Parker, clearly, was one of those individuals.

Another western expression to describe the drive to finish what's been started is 'she has no quit,' which means she'll never give up.

Denise Parker had no quit. Her father had discovered this, after he'd brought Denise a two-wheel bicycle when she was six years old. Denise raced up, jumped on the bike and rode off before Earl had even started to mount training wheels on the bike. Denise had no inkling how to stop the bike—there'd been no opportunity for her father to explain the finer points of braking —but that didn't stop Denise. Down the street she rode, perfectly balanced upon the bike, until she was almost out of sight. Anyone who saw the girl would have said she was doing fine.

Fine, that is, except for the small matter of the brakes.

She'd had no 'quit' when her shoe flew off during the foot race. She'd displayed grit aplenty as a seven year old with a 3-iron, which isn't a driver by any means, and yet drove a golf ball one hundred yards. She showed sand by working and working until she could dribble a basketball, without losing it, through a maze of plastic cones.

Denise Parker had no quit. This quality would serve her well for many years.

A Teenage Archer's Quest for Olympic Glory

The Dream

Denise had her share of dreams, both large and small. She dreamed, for instance, of going to the Olympics before she was old enough to understand what the Olympics were or what they entailed. Back then, when she was still enamored with running, her goal was to compete in either track or long-distance running. At the time, she hadn't even heard of archery, the event at which she'd one day dazzle the world.

Had Denise confided her Olympic dream to anyone other than her parents, she probably would have been advised to scale down her dreams; that the Olympics were great, but they were far beyond the reach of a youngster, from a decidedly middle-class family that hailed from South Jordan, Utah.

Becoming an Olympian, in any discipline, would involve time and money. Time was on Denise's side. Money wasn't. But what Denise didn't know could not affect her dreams.

So, she thought about being an Olympian and her parents might have thought about it, too. Had they really taken time to consider the idea, however, would Denise have gone on to achieve what she did? Had the Parkers really thought about it dispassionately they would have realized that fulfilling their daughter's dream would require money for coaching, money for travel and even more money for equipment. Had they done so they might easily have decided that any attempt to make Denise a world-class athlete capable of competing at the highest level of any sport they might have decided such an attempt would be well beyond their means.

They would have been right, too.

As it was, ignorance of what the future held was bliss. The Parkers simply took each day as it came, and cleared each obstacle in its turn, like the hurdler who refuses to worry about all the jumps because he's too busy concentrating on each one as he's approaching it.

That is exactly what Denise Parker and her parents did and how they approached her dream of one day competing in the Olympics. This is how their daughter's Olympic dream became reality sooner than anyone, Denise included, ever thought it would, and in a manner unlike any the Parkers could have anticipated. ■

Chapter 2
An Unusual Talent: Archery—What's That?

An Introduction to Archery

Earl Parker probably watched Denise at play on more than one occasion and wondered, is there anything the child **won't** try?

Denise Parker was petite. She was lean and fit, but no one would have called her muscular, at least not in the classic sense of the term. Few people simply looking at her would have guessed that she'd one day become a world class athlete. Yet within her beat the heart of a champion—and she had a mindset to match.

One day, in 1983, Earl decided to learn how to bow hunt. He knew very little about bows or how to shoot them, but he learned quickly and thought he'd give bowhunting a try.

Earl had grown up hunting with a rifle. But the places he enjoyed hunting seemed to become more crowded each year. Bowhunting requires the skill to slip up quite close to an animal before one shoots. Bowhunters need more patience and a steadier hand than is required when hunting with a rifle. Rifle hunting is considered much easier than bowhunting, which is why there are more rifle hunters in the U.S. than bowhunters. Earl, however, had never backed down from a challenge, and he thought this one might be especially enjoyable if for no other reason than he'd probably encounter fewer hunters come archery season.

Earl went shopping for a bow and returned with a compound bow and some matched arrows. Finding a place to practice was simple. He stacked straw bales in the family's backyard, and positioned a paper target against the bales. If Parker became as proficient with the bow as he hoped, he would use the bow to hunt elk that autumn.

Ever curious, particularly about sports, Denise was enthralled by her father's new bow. She wanted to see how shooting a bow would feel, and then watch as her arrows sunk deep into the bull's eye, or the innermost yellow circle on the target's face. The girl's quiet confidence led her to believe that she'd conquer archery as easily, quickly and thoroughly as she had other sports, and she couldn't wait to start.

Part of her curiosity may have been a natural offshoot of the strange, almost otherworldly appearance of her father's compound bow.

A compound bow looks strange for some very good reasons. Although a compound bow shoots arrows in the same general manner as a traditional longbow or recurved bow, the compound is radically different. A traditional bow is simplicity itself to look at; a compound, however, is constructed to use an intricate system of steel cables and cams designed to provide the archer with a mechanical advantage.

Pull back or draw any bow's string—and the energy from your body is transferred and stored in the bow's limbs. Release the string and most of that stored energy propels the arrow toward its target. Traditional bows had a simple cause-and-effect action that was easily understood: pull back the string, release the string. Pulling back the string—known as drawing the bow string—meant pulling and holding the total amount of latent force contained in the bow's flexed limbs until the archer reached 'full draw' the point at which the bow is said to be at its maximum potential power stroke.

An archer who pulls back on a compound's bow string will find that the string will reach a point, about halfway to full draw, when the bow's limbs suddenly relax. Depending on how the bow was engineered, once that point has been reached the archer gets a break. The bow's cables and cams, working in concert, now control part of the bow's latent force. When the bow's cams rolled over, it immediately became easier to pull back the string to full draw. Depending on the bow's configuration, an archer at full draw will be holding only between 20- and 50-percent of any compound bow's actual draw weight. Compound bows provide archers with a means of reducing the physical stress of drawing a bow and holding at full draw more efficient than any in history. When the string is released, however, the arrow will speed toward the target at a far greater velocity than that which should have been generated by the actual weight the archer was holding at full draw. That velocity, which is a function of the foot pounds of energy stored in the bow's limbs and transmitted to the arrow, is highly dependent upon the types of cams used in the bow's construction, a point we won't belabor here.

A compound bow, in addition to being a weird looking contraption, is also the most revolutionary development in archery's more than 30,000- year history.

This explanation of how a compound bow works is quite simplistic but perhaps it will provide you with some idea of a compound's somewhat strange appearance as well as a little about what advantages a compound bow imparts to its archer. The explanation may also help to explain Denise's fascination with her father's new bow.

One day, when Earl was asleep, Denise noticed his bow lying nearby. She wandered over to get a closer look, admired its cables, cams, limbs and string and thought how cool the bow was.

She then picked it up—she'd seen her father shoot so she had a vague idea of what to do—but although she tried to draw the bow string, she couldn't even budge it.

She was still struggling with the bow and string when her father awoke. Earl considered the scene briefly, and then asked, "How would you like to go shooting?"

Denise couldn't believe her good fortune.

Earl gathered up wife and daughter, loaded gear and family in the vehicle and then drove to a Salt Lake City archery range. Earl had been planning to take bowhunting lessons for his elk hunt anyway, and Denise's interest gave the man a pretense to get started immediately. His wife and daughter, meanwhile, would be learning the basics of target archery. The archery shop rented Denise and Valerie wooden recurved bows to use for their first lesson.

The First Lesson

Fred Jepson, of Salt Lake City, gave Denise her first lesson. Denise watched and waited while Jepson worked with her father. After a while the girl finally worked up the nerve to ask Jepson how she would go about shooting an arrow from her bow.

Jepson and Denise sat down and discussed archery for about 30 minutes. Then Denise took her first shot from a distance of 10 yards.

"I remember the first time (Jepson) put the bow in my hand," remembered Denise. "He said 'Pull it back,' and then, 'Let it go.'" Denise didn't know which hand she should pull back with, nor with which she should to let go. She'd observed arrows hurtling off other archers' bow strings and worried that somehow her own arrow might fly back and hit her in the face. She was relieved when her fears proved unfounded.

Denise Parker's first time shooting a bow wasn't at all noteworthy.

"I didn't display much talent at first," she said. Denise didn't, in fact, always hit the target she was aiming at—the one at the end of her shooting lane. Her arrow instead would sometimes hit the target in the shooting lane to the right, an occurrence the girl found extremely frustrating.

My Mom, Dad and I used to go rifle hunting for deer prior to taking up archery.

"I was listening to what the instructor said, but you never would have known it. He'd tell me, 'Aim by looking down the arrow.' I'd try, but my shots often veered off and hit to the right of the target I was aiming at.

"My instructor had seen other beginners do the exact thing many times before," explained Denise. Although the girl was naturally right-handed, she had a dominant left eye. That meant her left eye would take precedence, while she was aiming, without her even being aware of what was happening. Since she was shooting right-handed, however, her arrow would fly off course.

"Try shooting left-handed," the instructor suggested. Experience had taught him that it's far easier for a left eye dominant archer to overcome the problem early in the process, by learning to shoot left-handed, than later when bad habits may already be thoroughly ingrained in her technique.

Denise didn't like the suggestion that she shoot left-handed. She'd always been right-handed, of course, and such a radical change didn't seem like something she'd simply be able to accomplish with little or no problem.

Even at the very start, however, the girl enjoyed the feeling of holding the bow in her hand. She liked listening to the way the arrows whizzed off of the string and how they thudded into the target downrange. Being unable to immediately master proper form or technique, and noticing that her arrows weren't always hitting where she'd aimed she decided then and there to work until she became a better shot. She decided to listen to the instructor and try shooting left-handed. To do so, however, meant she must switch to shooting a left-handed bow.

Shooting left-handed was awkward for the youngster at first. Her right arm was stronger, naturally, since that was the dominant hand. Although pulling the string with her left hand was somewhat difficult it became easier to do so with practice.

Denise later understood why her instructor was so insistent that the girl switch her handedness, when shooting archery, to that of her dominant eye. "Shooting archery felt somewhat awkward even when I drew with my right arm," she said. "It didn't feel much more awkward with the left, so I was able to simply proceed from there like any other beginner."

The human body and its systems adapt to change much more readily than most people think they will. So it was with Denise. Shooting left-handed soon felt natural to her. That she also saw immediate improvement in her shooting was an unexpected bonus.

Two months later, Denise's arrow would regularly be penetrating a 60-centimeter target at a distance of 18 meters, or slightly more than 60 feet.

In the Beginning . . .

"We always taught Denise she could do anything she set her mind to do," Valerie Parker said. "We taught her about goals, perseverance and never giving in. Winning doesn't count nearly as much as putting forth the effort." The Parkers also took the time to explain the differences between short-range goals and long-range goals and the secret of achieving them, namely, take it one day at a time.

For her part, Denise knows she was luckier than many youngsters in having parents who valued her for who she was, not what she did. The Parkers had no expectations of their daughter.

Denise didn't have her own bow for quite some time. She knew that to become a better archer she had to practice regularly, and yet the only nearby team that shot on a weekly basis was The Utah Wheelchair Archers, so she began shooting with them.

"What made me a good archer right away was a desire to improve and an ability to understand exactly what my instructors were trying to explain," said Denise. "My goal, from the very first, was to develop perfect shooting form and technique. I'd apply what I'd learned to each shot I took. The other kids worried about where their arrows hit; I never did as much. I just continued to work on improving my form and technique, the basics of shooting archery, and in a matter of weeks I was the best shooter on the team. I knew that the accuracy would come."

Denise had a natural aptitude for playing sports which, like archery, required superb eye-hand coordination. She believes that while some people must labor to develop great eye-hand coordination, hers was innate. As was her natural ability to focus on something to the exclusion of all else. The best archers seek to acquire or improve both of these attributes because they are of inestimable value to the competitive archer. As she worked to become a better archer, Denise was also improving the synchronization of eye with hand and sharpening her focus until it would become almost laser-like in its intensity.

Budd Rose, a local instructor, helped me a lot during the first years of shooting.

Several other able-bodied youngsters joined the Utah Wheelchair Archers soon after Denise had started shooting with the group. Having more 'bodies' around meant that the formation of a new archery club had become possible. That club—the Utah Hot Shots—was also a JOAD—Junior Olympic Archery Development club. The designation refers to an affiliation with the National Archery Association, the U.S. Olympic archery program's governing body.

Not until the girl learned about JOAD and its relationship to the Hot Shots did she realize that archery was an Olympic sport. She'd shot arrows mainly because she enjoyed doing so before then. But since she'd always wanted to compete in the Olympics she now attacked archery practice with new fervor. If she became a good enough shot, archery might become her ticket to Olympic competition.

Some people think athletic talent is a matter of being lucky enough to get the right genes. Denise doesn't buy into that theory.

"Of course in any sport you have to have some level of natural ability, but determination and drive play a huge role in success," explained Denise. "I'm not necessarily the 'ideal physical' specimen for my sport, but practice and hard work can overcome many physical limitations."

"Becoming involved with the Utah Hot Shots really helped me develop my potential in archery," said Denise. She explained that Randi and Larry Smith, the instructors for the club, not only provided instruction, but also created a fun environment. Going to the club provided the girl with needed social structure, a competitive environment that spurred her ever onward, and continuing instruction, all of which helped Denise to flourish as an archer.

Denise improved despite the lack of a nationally-known archery instructor. "Most archers who take lessons from any archery instructor who's good at what he or she does will continue to get better," explained Denise. "In the beginning, my instructors weren't well-known outside of Salt Lake City, but they prevented me from developing the bad habits that might have destroyed my career before it ever got started."

By the time she was ten, Denise had settled down nicely into archery even thought archery was unlike anything she'd ever tried before. Soccer and basketball appealed to her because of their physicality. The girl simply loved to kick a soccer ball or shoot baskets for hours on end.

"I can't say I loved archery right away," commented Denise. "It was hard not having my other friends participate in it with me. I did, however, love shooting arrows. There is something magical about releasing the string and propelling an arrow towards a target." Denise also enjoyed working to improve her technique, but not the incredibly long hours of practice sometimes required. Practice, however, was a means to an end.

Once the rookie archer had been shooting for just a short time she discovered she became hooked on the sport. "Each shot was exciting. I'd pull back and the arrow would shoot off the string so quickly it always came as a surprise."

She was now hitting what she aimed at, too; which was another reason to be excited about the sport.

Denise found she was growing to love the sport, but for the longest while she couldn't figure out exactly why. "I knew it wasn't just about shooting arrows, for the ribbons and trophies," said the woman. "Then one day, I knew exactly why I loved archery so — it was for the competition and the winning.

"Archery lit my competitive fire like no other sport I'd ever tried, before or since," Denise concluded. "Unlike team sports where you have to depend on others to win, in archery you could determine your own destiny. If you were good enough to win, nothing could get in your way." ■

Chapter 3

I Have Potential!

The Flickering Flame

Anyone who has ever belonged to a scouting or campfire organization, gone overnight camping with parents or friends, or attended homecoming activities or pep rallies where bonfires were part of the celebration knows such huge, planned fires don't just happen. Instead, much preparation goes into the construction of such a blaze. Creating a fire large enough to inspire team spirit, feelings of great friendship and even awe isn't as easy as one might imagine. The construction of such a conflagration, or fire, one whose spectacular orange tongues of flame leap high into the darkening sky while the burning wood hisses and crackles, takes work, and lots of it.

The feeling in Denise Parker's gut, as she slowly realized that competitive archery might be a sport at which she could excel, could be likened to that flickering flame. As the youngster practiced dutifully, both in her backyard and with the Utah Hot Shots, she got an inkling of what might someday be possible. Her Olympic dream, once clearly a long shot possibility even to her, clarified as she turned her attention to archery. The thought of possibly one day achieving status as a world-class archer served as the dry kindling that fed the figurative flame in the girl's gut. Denise had no way of knowing that within the space of a few short years that flame would attain bonfire-sized heat, mass and intensity.

Keeping the flame going, however, during those early days,

My Mom and I frequently shot together. She is shooting a compound bow and I have a recurve bow.

months and years while Denise learned everything she could about archery would be critical. The trick for anyone serious about competing is to work, work and work some more, to practice and improve until one becomes the best one can possibly be, yet to accomplish this task without burning out.

Bonfire builders, for example, work strenuously in an attempt to create the biggest, hottest and most tremendous fire they and their audience have ever seen. But when all fuel or wood has been used up and the fire-tenders become too fatigued to gather more, then the fire will gradually burn down into ash and eventually go out.

So, too, it often is with an athlete or scholar who, early on, stokes the flames of enthusiasm until white hot, but is then unable to maintain such a high degree of intensity. That's when the very sport or subject that once engaged that person's mind, heart and soul becomes an object of drudgery, one the athlete or scholar can barely think about much less willingly perform. That's called 'burn out,' and it is much more common than one might suppose, even in professional athletes.

Young tennis phenomenon Jennifer Capriati 'burned out' when barely into her teens. Capriati had been a rising star before she quit tennis completely for a couple of years in an attempt to live a normal life. After a time, however, she realized that tennis was in her soul and returned to the sport in which her star had been ascendant at the time of her temporary retirement. Professional bass angler Roland Martin has made an excellent living from fishing tournaments, starring in and producing fishing videos and hosting a TV fishing show. Martin did well because he loved fishing; at least he did at first. Later, however, if you were to corner the man in hopes of discussing fishing, he much preferred talking about turkey hunting. When asked why, he replied that he'd had to fish for so many years, even when he didn't want to, that much of his enthusiasm for the sport had simply disappeared.

Each day, as young Parker headed out into her backyard to practice, or journeyed for another session with the Hot Shots, she ran the risk of becoming bored or even training too diligently or hard. Denise shot a lot—10 hours or more each week, which is a lot for an 11 year old, but never lost her fascination with archery nor the desire to improve.

"Every night we would shoot six to ten arrows, pull them out of the target, then return (to the firing line) and shoot again," Earl Parker recalled. "I imagine it got pretty boring for (Denise), yet she'd never want to stop. She always wanted to shoot more."

Denise Parker may have been an 11-year-old, but she already had a goal. That goal was being fueled by the flame that smoldered in the girl's heart and mind, soul and gut.

The flickering flame is crucial to a budding athlete's love of her sport and, consequently, her eventual success. But as bonfires must be tended carefully, so must the flame of competition lest it flickers and dies. Conversely, a fire that flares up too brightly during its earliest stages may sometimes use up its fuel and expire. When that occurs it's often said that 'the fire consumed itself.'

Tending the flickering flame of competition is never an easy task. And when the goal is a lofty one, such as the desire to become a world-class participant, it's even more difficult. From the moment that Denise Parker felt the start of that fire, from the instant Earl and Valerie Parker grasped the reality of their daughter's still untapped potential, and from whenever the first of Denise's many accomplished archery instructors glimpsed

My Dad and me outside our RV during an archery hunt.

greatness within her, an almost infinite number of pitfalls could have been tumbled into that easily might have ended everything. Those pitfalls were wide-ranging and consisted of obstacles both real and imagined, potential stumbling blocks occasionally so daunting to a would-be competitor as to have caused the end of many a promising sports or academic career before it ever really began.

Walking a Fine Line

Denise Parker's coaches had to have been aware, if only subconsciously, of what it would take—what incredible sacrifices would be called for, and at almost every level—during the time needed to mold a rookie 11-year-old archer into a rising archery star. Long-time coaches usually know, in a way that a young competitor and her parents can't yet comprehend, that maintaining an athlete's interest in a sport while she diligently labored to transform natural talent into a level of skill high enough to send her soaring through archery's competitive ranks, would mean walking a fine line indeed.

No one needed to remind the Parkers or the coaches who'd contributed to their daughter's training that Denise was only a child and remained a student in nearby Welby Elementary School. She had friends with whom she still played sports, Bonzo, her dog, with whom she'd run to give exercise, and the studies she enthusiastically embraced. Denise was a happy, All-American girl. The idea was to keep her that way, whether or not she one day developed into a super archer.

The first steps along the path to archery success had been taken, but hidden obstacles loomed, including the much-feared burn out, which was discussed earlier. The term 'burn out' may not have been quite as common in the mid-1980s as it is today, and that could have been a problem. And yet coaches have always known of talented athletes who, whether through mental or physical fatigue or a fear of letting others down, abandoned their sports, never to return. Burn out was to be feared, and everyone but Denise probably realized it.

Burn out remained a consideration, especially during Denise's earliest years in archery, as those around her were still assessing the depths of the youngster's desire. It was, however, the last thing on anyone's mind in 1985, with the Weber Invitational Archery Tournament looming first on one weekend and the Utah State Archery Championships the next. ■

Chapter 4
My First Competition

Starting Out Small

The Weber Invitational would be Denise's first official competition, which probably was a good thing. "Only two of us were in my class, designated for kids aged 12 and under," Denise recalled. As she waited for the event to begin the tiny blonde archer couldn't help but eye her taller, stronger, male competition.

"This boy had it all," recalled Denise. "The best and newest gear: compound bow, telescopic bow-sights, a mechanical release (compound bow archers often use a mechanical bowstring release rather than their fingers to release bow-strings), everything you could imagine.

"I had a recurve because that's the only kind of bow competitors are allowed to shoot in the Olympics. Which are much simpler, traditional bows."

Denise had believed herself fairly well prepared and yet the boy out shot her by "a lot of points," as she later would note.

Rather than simply call it quits, after this rather thorough thrashing, Denise became fired up.

"I got mad that he beat me," she said. "I became furious with myself, even though it was my first tournament and (I had a serious equipment disadvantage). I came home and told my Dad that I wanted all that (same) stuff on my bow."

The fishing trip that the Parkers had planned to take was put on hold while Denise prepared to do whatever was necessary to even the playing field with the boy who had beaten her.

Getting Mad, Getting Even

Denise and Earl decided to visit Bob 'Jake' Jacobson, proprietor of Jake's Archery Shop in Orem, Utah.

"Jake was said to be the best person in the area for getting bows properly set up and giving lessons," explained Denise.

Denise wanted all the bells and whistles too, but a recurve isn't 'high tech' like a compound bow is. In other words, there's just so much equipment-wise one can do to improve a recurve's performance. That, however, Jacobson was willing and able to do.

"Jake rigged my bow with a peep sight," Denise said. "Which is all I really could add to my recurve, and he also gave me a couple of private archery lessons while we were there."

A peep sight forces an archer to focus complete attention on the target. Black and shaped like a doughnut, an archer 'peeps' through the sight's doughnut hole to assure the sight's proper alignment with the target before she releases the bowstring. A peep sight and some lessons may not sound like much, to anyone unfamiliar with

My first tournament—The Weber State Invitational.

A Teenage Archer's Quest for Olympic Glory

bows or recurves, but it proved more than enough. Of course, redoubling her practice efforts that week helped as well.

The next weekend at the Utah State Championships, still with her recurve bow, Denise faced the same boy, together with other competitors and beat them all.

Denise's first Utah state competition was when it dawned on the girl that she might actually be a pretty good archer on a local level. At least on a local level.

My parents and me at a Junior Olympic Archery Development (JOAD) Tournament.

Nationals

The Parker camp, which included Denise, was to learn a good deal more about the youngster and the depths of her resolve during her first national competition in Las Vegas, Nevada, at an event now known as The World Archery Festival. Denise would be competing against a number of highly-ranked junior archers.

Denise remembers vividly her first two arrows of the match.

"I was 11-years-old and extremely nervous," explained Denise. "My first arrow missed the entire target, which was so devastating that I began to cry. My parents tried to comfort me, but it was pretty devastating."

Denise eventually regained her poise and steadied her nerves. At the end of the competition she'd finished fourth out of the ten competitors in her division. Despite a momentary flirtation with disaster, in the end the youngster prevailed. The strong finish inspired hope that she might do even better in future events.

Denise Parker

My parents and I would shoot in a local archery tournament almost every weekend.

She became a familiar face at local archery tournaments and state JOAD contests as she began accumulating the first of many ribbons, medals and trophies that would one day comprise an enviable memorabilia collection. Each new competition netted the young archer an intangible reward more valuable than ribbons or medals, and that was experience.

Earl and Valerie traveled everywhere with their daughter, sometimes the elder Parkers joined Denise in competitions, but in their own divisions.

Denise's parents loved the competition and loved the fact that they could all compete. It was fun to do together. The family's exceptional closeness and parents' willingness to allow Denise to go as far, competitively, as she could were of primary importance during the youngster's future and unprecedented surge into the forefront of American competitive archery. ∎

Chapter 5
Winning!

Winning isn't the main thing . . .
In July, 1985, Denise was the ripe old age of 11. The National Junior Olympic Archery Development Championships was her primary focus as she continued taking lessons and shooting hundreds of practice arrows each week. The girl's confidence was high since she'd been given additional instruction by Budd Rose, another fine local instructor. Her principal and most dedicated coach, however, was her dad. Denise trusted Earl and knew he had her best interests at heart. The situation, luckily, suited father and daughter equally well.

Denise's shooting accomplishments next led to a two-week stay at a Junior Archery Development (JOAD) camp slated to be held that summer at Miami University, in Oxford, Ohio. Attendees would be schooled in various aspects of competitive shooting while well away from any sources of distraction. JOAD camp marked the first time Denise would be gone from home for any length of time. As most of us can attest, going away to camp can be quite traumatic. Denise, however, mustn't have received that news update. Or, perhaps, the girl's single-minded dedication to the honing of her competitive *persona* had become so all-consuming she had little time to miss her home, her parents or much of anything else.

Devotion paid off when she finished second that year and returned the following year at age 12 to win the National JOAD Championships. Competitors shoot 144 arrows, or 36 arrows at each of four distances: 20 meters (a meter is slightly longer than a yard), 30, 40 and 50 meters. Archers from across the country, as well as 15 other countries, were vying for the first place medal. Denise solidified her burgeoning reputation as 'the one to beat' by winning the junior girls' championship.

It was now time to turn her sights to the next major national competition, the National Indoor Championships to be held in April at the Olympic Training Center in Colorado Springs.

Again, Denise captured first at the Indoor Championships beginning her reign as the U.S. Junior Women's Indoor Archery Champion. Even more remarkably, the girl from South Jordan, Utah's overall score of 1,126 trumped the 1,124 score shot by the senior champion, who was then rewarded with the title, National Women's Indoor Champion, despite having scored two points less than the junior champion, Denise.

Had Denise been registered in the senior division as well as the junior bracket she would have worn both crowns—junior and

Here I am at the Olympic Training Center when I was about 11 years old.

senior women's. Since she'd entered the junior event only, that title was the only one to which she could lay claim.

Denise's cumulative score that day broke the existing junior women's record, which meant her score was higher than any ever shot by a U.S. female 18 years of age and younger. The girl also broke three national age-class records—at 18 meters, 25 meters and in the JOAD category—while shooting FITA I and FITA II rounds*.

At the time, she stood 4 feet 10 inches tall, in her stocking feet, and weighed 72 pounds, soaking wet. The diminutive youngster had found her niche, however, and now found neither junior nor senior competitors at any level the least bit daunting. Fearfulness, it seemed, wasn't a part of her emotional make-up.

Both of these wins qualified Denise to become a member of the U. S. Junior Olympic Elite Archery Team. Later in the year, team members would be able to gain valuable experience as they practiced with the nation's top archers, members of the U. S. Olympic Senior Archery Team.

Although shooting a bow was something for which the youngster had tremendous talent, by no means was archery the only thing in Denise's life. She belonged to a local softball team and had been named to their league's all-star team. She played golf, soccer and basketball, too. Most importantly her grade point average never dipped any lower than 3.7, or a solid A+.

What Next?

One national indoor archery champion, age 13. Potential: limitless. Had Earl and Valerie Parker taken out a classified ad stating the above the pair couldn't have attracted more attention.

"Once I'd won at Colorado Springs people started giving my parents advice about my career," said Denise. "One would say, 'Do this,' while the next would advise, 'No, do that.' It was very confusing, and for quite some time."

The family's understandable frustration over which way to turn next ended when Rick McKinney approached Earl to discuss Denise's future in archery. McKinney, a former world champion archer who'd already competed in two Olympics, was well-regarded in the world of archery. Earl eagerly listened as McKinney stated he thought Denise was shooting well enough to qualify for the 1988 Olympic archery team.

The Olympics had always been the girl's goal, but no one—including the Parkers—ever expected that she might be able to compete as early as 1988. The archer would be 18 in 1992, and so she and her parents naturally thought those would be the first Games in which she might compete. The 1988 Games hadn't even been considered an option since Denise would be just 14-years-old at the time.

McKinney's assessment of Denise's competitive talents was based upon a number of factors. First, her amazing performance at the National Indoor Championships where she astounded casual observers and professional archers alike with her focus and drive as well as her dedication to practice and the near-constant refinements of her form and technique. But also the inner-drive he saw in her. She seemed to be willing to do anything to win.

McKinney, however impressed he might have been with the youngster's titles and honors, had, if not 'bigger fish to fry,' then certainly bigger fish-fries to plan.

"The Pan American Games Trials will be held this summer (1987)," said McKinney. "Denise should try to make the team."

Flattered as they were by the man's enthusiasm and stellar opinion of their daughter's talent and skill, the Parkers said, 'no.' They felt they had no alternative but to do so due to financial worries.

A Teenage Archer's Quest for Olympic Glory

Rick McKinney wouldn't take 'no' for an answer. "Put Denise on a plane (to Phoenix, where the qualifying match would be held) and I'll take care of the rest," he assured the Parkers.

Such an offer was tempting, no doubt about it. But naturally the Parker's worried about sending Denise alone. And yet the Parkers wouldn't have trusted just anyone with their daughter. Rick McKinney, however, assured the Parker's that their daughter was safe and that this was an event that their daughter had to attend. They were proud that McKinney perceived something special about their daughter, perhaps the same things that they and the girl's previous coaches had discerned. McKinney's opinion, they believed, had been swayed not only by the tangible trappings of their daughter's success, like trophies and titles, but the intangibles—things that couldn't be seen—as well, Denise's fearlessness and drive and perseverance. The Parkers, realizing that McKinney had offered their young daughter the chance of a lifetime, now acted on faith and hoped—and prayed — that no matter what the result, it would be the best thing for Denise.

Me and Rick McKinney in 1986.

Preparation

McKinney's offer caused the Parker household to erupt in a chain reaction of activity once the family had returned home. At the close of each business day, or about 3:00 p.m., Parker would hurry to pick up Denise and the two would then drive to Budd Rose's house where the man would give the girl private archery instructions. An additional advantage of practicing at Budd's was the man's 70 meter outdoor range, one of the distances archers must shoot in both the Pan American Games and the Trials.

Denise now increased the time she spent practicing each day. She trained with free weights, did aerobic exercises and ran long distances regularly. And at the same time, continued to participate in organized sports at school. Her schedule was so busy that April—and its Phoenix departure date—seemed to creep up on her before she was fully ready for it.

The drive to the airport was a sad one. "My Mom cried the entire way," Denise recalled. "She worried about sending her 'baby—me—off to join Rick McKinney and Sherri Rhodes, another Olympic archery coach, where she would have no idea of what was happening."

Valerie knew Rick and Sherri were respected in the industry. She also was aware that everyone spoke highly of them. Like all human mothers fearful of placing their young in danger's way, Valerie reacted with worry, trepidation and tears.

How difficult it must have been for young Denise to walk away from her weeping mother, coach-father, home and all she held dear. Yet so great was the girl's desire to compete that she shed a few tears of her own, kissed Valerie good-bye, boarded the plane and embarked upon a future far beyond anything she might have imagined just a few short years before.

Life in Phoenix

The not-quite five-foot-tall Denise watched the women—*women!*—against whom she'd be competing and felt something she'd felt only rarely before: intimidation.

A Teenage Archer's Quest for Olympic Glory

"I felt out of place," she admitted. "I not only was, by far, the youngest person competing there, my competition, for the first time, was made up of only much older women. Those women would also be shooting bows with almost twice the draw weight of my bow." 'Draw weight' is the amount of limb and string resistance an archer must overcome when coming to full draw. An archer who shoots a 50-pound recurve, for example, must pull back and actually hold 50 pounds of pressure.

Denise started out with an 18-pound recurve bow. As she grew and added muscle she progressed to a 20-pound bow. In Phoenix, she would be using a 25-pound recurve, quite a substantial bow for a girl of her size, and yet most of her competitors would be shooting 35- to 45-pound bows.

Denise would gain no advantage from the lighter draw-weight bow. Twenty-five pounds of draw weight was all she could realistically hope to handle without sacrificing accuracy. Her bow proportionately was as difficult for her to draw as the heavier draw weight bows were for the older women. All competitors would probably be equally fatigued at the end of a day of shooting.

The bow's disadvantages, however, were daunting. A woman wielding a 40-pound draw weight bow would shoot arrows having a much flatter trajectory. Trajectory can be defined as the curve, or arc, in the arrow's flight path as it travels from the bow to its first point of impact. The trajectory of an arrow shot from a bow with a draw weight of 40-pounds or more will be much flatter than that of an arrow shot from a bow with 25-pounds of draw weight.

In other words, her competitors' arrows would slam into the targets on a flight path nearly horizontal to the earth. Denise's arrows entered with fletching or feathers pointing skyward, since their trajectories caused them to fall into the target from that direction. Such a high trajectory makes arrows more susceptible to wind and weather conditions—meaning that the wind can move the arrows away from the target much easier.

Adding to the youngster's woes was the chore of putting up targets on the mat, or backstop, at the end of her 70 meter lane. Denise was willing to do so, and yet far too short to reach the top of the targets.

"I'd have to ask one of my competitors to help me 'pin' up my target," she explained. "It just added to the feeling that maybe I didn't belong there."

The Competition

Denise was intelligent as well as sensitive. She understood immediately that many of the women she was competing against were less than thrilled to be lumped together with a 13-year-old.

"I don't know whether they resented me because of my age or because of how well I could shoot," Denise commented. "I just knew some of them didn't like me."

Had several women not been willing to take her under their wings, the Pan American Trials might have been an extremely lonely, intense and trying experience. But thanks to Luann Ryon, the 1976 U. S. Olympic gold medalist (recently back

Trena King and me having fun on the range.

in action after a two year retirement), Judy Adams, favored to win the 1980 Moscow Olympics (had they not been boycotted by the U. S.), and Trena King, the experience ended up quite rewarding.

"These three women were wonderful to me," said Denise. "They seemed happy I was there. I think they enjoyed watching an accomplished, young shooter moving up through the ranks. They treated me like one of their own, joking about my hair, my clothes or boys. They discussed things teenagers usually like to talk about and that put me at ease."

"Luann was so unique," explained Denise. "She gave me a new perspective on competition. Every time she'd step off the shooting the line she'd smile happily, even if she'd just shot poorly. I asked why she did this, and she replied, 'Because the others (competitors) will never know what I'm thinking when they see me smiling like this.' Just seeing that big smile on Luann's face, she'd calculated, might be enough to throw some competitors off their A games."

Dealing With It!

She stepped up for the first time on the firing line and, for an instant, doubts assailed her. Her age, size—her bow was 3 inches taller than she was—the bow's light draw weight, severely arcing trajectories, lighter arrows more prone to wind drift, everything entered the teenager's mind in those moments. "I knew I could shoot arrows," explained Denise. That was probably the saving grace of everything. Even though I had a lot of emotion running through my body and quite frankly, I didn't start the event off that well. I had confidence in my ability to shoot arrows into the middle of the target."

Denise remained quite comfortable in her own skin, and convinced of her own special abilities. "I'm lucky, I guess," she said. I just had an inner-confidence about my ability and knew that it would all work out."

Denise Parker

The Trials

The Pan American Trials were to last four days. By the time they ended, the four top-scoring women and four top-scoring men would have earned slots on the U. S. archery team. That team would represent the U. S. at the Pan American Games, which would be held that summer in Indianapolis.

To qualify, each archer must shoot 144 arrows per day at a distance of 70, 60, 50 and 30 meters. There were no age groups and no divisions except that women shot against women and men against men.

Denise didn't shoot well at first. Her name wasn't on the leader board after the conclusion of the first two distances. By the end of the first day, however, she'd moved into second place.

"I then settled down and shot quite well," Denise said, in something of an understatement.

Sixty nationally-ranked U. S. women archers competed in Phoenix that spring. Somewhat surprisingly, considering the caliber of the competition, the 13-year-old outshot all of them. Denise won the event, and a place on the U.S. Pan American Team, with a score of 2,498 out of a possible 2,880. The other women's team members were Luann Ryon, Trena King and Michelle Borders, who finished second with a score of 2,470, or 28 points fewer than Denise.

By winning the Pan Am Trials, Denise had moved a step closer to her goal. She'd also positioned herself among the nation's foremost female archers and was perfectly placed to be considered for a berth on the 1988 U.S. Olympic Team which would represent the country in Seoul, South Korea.

The Pressure Builds

It's one thing to start out at age 11 as a complete unknown and then fly beneath the competitive radar during one's earliest competitions. Not to be too dramatic, but when 13-year-old Denise went up against the country's top senior women archers and emerged the clear winner the pressure on the girl must have been extreme. And yet she'd done the unimaginable, the almost incomprehensible, and the eyes of the world were now upon her. Could she even bear up to the heavy mantle of expectations that suddenly seemed to press in on her from all directions?

Denise may have been small but she feared no one and lived only to win. And that is a dangerous combination.

Dangerous, perhaps, and yet relatively unseasoned despite the titles she kept accumulating.

"I'd started working around this time with another superb archery coach, Tim Strickland, then living in Little Rock, Arkansas," Denise said. "Tim had seen me shoot in Las Vegas after my Dad asked him to come watch me.

"'Do you think she has potential?' Dad asked.

Tim replied, 'Tremendous potential.'

That was good enough for my dad. After Dad and Tim discussed my future prospects, I'd train with Tim whenever possible."

Flights to Little Rock, Arkansas, trips to national competitions, money for travel, lodging and food, often for parents, coach and competitor, soon put a serious crimp in the Parkers' budget. Along the way—and because, like most top competitors of the day, Denise shot arrows manufactured by Easton Aluminum—the company agreed to sponsor the girl to help defray her expenses.

"Jim Easton was passionate about the Olympics," explained Denise. "It was important to Jim that the U.S. do well, but especially in archery." Knowing that Denise was one of his country's main archery hopes, Easton decided to foot Denise's travel bills so that she could train in Little Rock with Strickland.

Denise would fly in to Little Rock where Tim or his wife, Shirley, would pick her up. She'd stay with the couple in their home and practice every day she was there.

"Tim would watch me shoot, provide me with pointers or instruction and then he'd video me shooting," said Denise. "I'd bring Tim's videos home and my Dad and I would watch them and that would help us work on my technique." To keep Strickland up to speed on how Denise was doing in Utah, Earl would video his daughter shooting and then mail the videos to Tim for comments.

Tim Strickland (my coach) and me working together.

To prepare for the Pan Am Games, Denise increased her practice time. She began shooting three or four hours a day, five or six days a week.

One could say that Denise Parker, even at age 13, truly had her eye on the prize.

Life at the Pan American Games

Denise Parker had traveled to many different competitions in her brief career. When she traveled to Indianapolis, however, to take part in the Pan American Games, she did so for the first time in the company of women, her U. S. archery teammates. She arrived there as one of the youngest of the more than 5,000 Pan Am athletes who had gathered for the competition, and as one of the United States' best and brightest hopes for a gold medal in both this and future competitions.

They arrived without incident in Indianapolis, Denise all the while doing her best to fit in with women much older than her. She deluded herself into believing that the women had accepted her, on every level, without question. Women, however, are as apt to pull pranks on the easily-fooled or the gullible among them as men, the more notorious pranksters. And these women had prepared a real 'doozy' to play on the youngster they affectionately referred to as 'Little Bit.'

"We'd no sooner arrived when my teammates told me we'd all have to get a sex test," Denise explained. "I didn't like the sound of that. It freaked me out, actually. I asked, 'What do they do in a sex test?' Someone—I don't remember who—said, 'They take you in a room and make certain that you're really a girl.'

"I was so upset thinking about this that when I went into the room, all worried, I didn't know what they would do. As it turned out, however, they only took a swab from the inside of my cheek.

"When I came back out, everyone was laughing. I had to join in—it was funny, thinking back on it, but at the time I remember thinking, 'You guys suck!'"

The women's team was joined by the men's team comprised of Ed Eliason, 49, Denise's fellow Utahan who worked for Easton Aluminum, the outfit that sponsored both. Eliason began shooting and winning at a young age too, just not quite as young as Denise had. At the age of 14, he won the Washington state title. He later would finish fifth in the 1972 Munich Summer Olympics and also qualified for the 1980 Moscow Olympics, which were boycotted by the U. S.

Eliason was full of praise for his young teammate. "She's the hottest thing in U. S. archery right now," he said to a reporter. He also noted that the girl was the youngest competitor ever to make it into archery's highest ranks.

Eliason may have been especially effusive—or full of praise, because at the Pan Am Trials the youngster had turned the tables, one might say, to help Eliason improve his game.

"I was moping around (in the Pan Am Trials) with a scowl on my face when I heard Denise say, 'Hey, dude, you're looking a little tight to me. Your release is coming out from your face and you're dropping your bow,' which meant my follow-through was poor. I worked on and improved those things and beat two of the best archers in the world—1984 Olympic silver medalist Rick McKinney and former Olympic gold medalist Darrell Pace."

Call it payback for the advice Eliason provided to the Parkers earlier that spring. "I suggested she increase her draw length from 22 inches to 23 inches," Eliason said. "(Her arrows) started to fly then. It's amazing how quickly she adapts to tactical (equipment) changes."

Ed Eliason joined Jay Barrs, Rick McKinney and Darrell Pace on the U. S. men's Pan Am archery team.

The Pan Am Games were to last a total of five days. On the event's opening qualification

Jim Easton and me. Without Jim's support, I don't know how I would have funded the travel and training it required.

round, the U. S. men's and women's archery teams made their presence known when they swept the first four places of the competition.

The format during the Pan Am Games final elimination round called for competitors to start out with 36 arrows, shooting nine of them, in sets of three, from each of four distances—30, 50, 60 and 70 meters for the women. Cuts would be made, depending on the outcome (scores) during each round, and surviving teams would shoot again.

Each would have two-and-a-half minutes to shoot her three arrows. Denise rarely used all of her time.

"I don't like spending a lot of time up there (on the firing line)," she said. "Never seemed to make much sense to just stand around between arrows. I just figured, get up there and shoot 'em. Maybe my age and care-free spirit contributed to this attitude."

By the end of the first day, Denise had moved into first place. She remained solidly in first after the second day, led for most of the third day and on the fourth and final elimination day, won the gold medal.

Denise had moved up to shoot a 28-pound bow at these Games. "If I (were drawing) more pounds, then my arrow would go flatter . . . to the target," she explained. "My arrow arcs or goes up more so the wind can affect it more."

Weather conditions during the games were hardly ideal, at least not for Denise and especially not in the finals when a tricky crosswind made accurate shooting, with a low draw weight bow, even more difficult than usual.

In the finals, Denise needed to shoot a score of 24 or better with her final three arrows to assure herself of the individual gold medal. A bulls-eye counts for 10 points, while each succeeding 'ring' counts for one point less. That's why the circle or ring closest to the bulls-eye is called the 'nine ring,' and the next is termed 'the

Luanne Ryon, Trena King and me getting ready for the medal ceremony at the 1987 Pan American Games.

eight ring,' etc., because each represents the number of points earned when an arrow lands within that ring.

The young archer stepped to the line on the 70 meter course, made two perfect bulls-eye shots and then slammed one home into the 'seven ring,' for a final score of 27, or three points more than what was needed.

"Before I shot each day, usually someone would try to talk to me about how I felt or how I'd performed the day before," Denise said. "I preferred not discussing it at all. My strategy was to focus on what I was doing and try not to get too excited by what might be possible."

Denise had 'zoned out,' as she always did, when the medal was on the line. She had a knack for focusing exclusively on the job at hand—archery—whenever she was competing. It made no difference who was nearby—and on this occasion Dad could not be at the competition so mom and her two step-brothers were there. But, only one thing mattered and that was making a bulls-eye.

When the final arrow had penetrated the target, the youngster

A Teenage Archer's Quest for Olympic Glory

Our team on the medal stand during the 1987 Pan American Games.

knew she'd won the individual gold to go along with the team gold medal previously captured by the American team of eight. Everyone was overwhelmed by Denise's stellar performance. "My parents were both very proud (of me)," Denise said. "I remember mom crying with joy. My dad was very disappointed that he had to stay home from the event to work and was not able to join in the excitement of the win."

Denise's total score was 315 of a possible 360, which won her the gold in individual competition. Finishing second was Trena King, of Michigan, who garnered 306 points, while Eva Bueno of Cuba won the bronze medal with a score of 297. Winning not one, but two golds, Denise shot her way into the history books as the youngest archer ever to capture these prizes in Pan American Games competition.

Luann Ryon, who roomed with Denise at the games, commented on the youngster's accomplishment. "What Denise has done is extraordinary," Ryon said. "We've had young kids shoot well before, but never this young and this well."

Ryon's personal best stood at 1,295; Denise's Pan Am total was 1,262, or just 33 points less than that of an Olympic gold medalist.

Denise may have been young and confident but she was also wise enough to say the right things in almost every situation. "I hope to be as good as Luann some day," Denise responded, when told of the relative closeness of their two scores.

Luann Ryon, known for smiling even when she wasn't doing well, had wanted to win this event, no question about it. So did Denise's two other teammates. They did whatever they could do, psychologically, and cut the youngster no slack at all. "We tease (Denise) and harass her a lot," Ryon commented at the time. "That can take a lot of people right out of their game. Not her, though. She just looks at you, laughs and wings her arrows down (to the target)."

Luann Ryon had been the queen of U. S. archery. The crowd at the Pan Am Games must have recognized that the results of this event signaled a change of reign. As the British say, upon the death of a ruling monarch, "The Queen is dead. Long live the Queen." Not to show disrespect to the former queen, but to acknowledge the continuity of succession, or of the country's rulers.

Luann Ryon, the queen, had possibly been deposed on this late summer day in 1987. A new queen—Denise Parker—may have been crowned. Long live the queen! ∎

Chapter 6
Dealing with Pressure

Single-Minded

Denise Parker won a Pan Am Games individual gold medal in archery and, by doing so, she'd breathed new life into archery, a sport many Americans had considered staid and even slightly stuffy. She was instantly celebrated as the 'little kid who could,' and many Americans, who previously had been disengaged in the selection of U.S. Olympic team members, now avidly devoured any news item in which Denise or archery were mentioned. Without intending to do so, Denise had become for many of her countrymen and women the living, breathing personification of something once said by the late Vince Lombardi, the Green Bay Packers' coach, "Winning isn't everything, it's the **ONLY** thing!"

Younger generations who were too young at the time or perhaps hadn't even been born may have difficulty comprehending the scope of the media frenzy that reported on Denise's every move. Nor will they probably understand the magnitude of what she was still trying to accomplish at an age younger than anyone else in the history of the sport. The teenager had beaten a sizable field consisting of older, more seasoned international competitors, to win Pan Am gold, yet still was too young by three years to be trusted with a bow-hunting license in her home state.

Despite ribbons, trophies and medals by the score, despite feats of archery skill that left coaches and onlookers breathless,

Denise remained a child, in both stature and age.

"I never thought of myself as being the best 13-year old archer," explained Denise. "I just wanted to be the best that I could be."

While others obsessed about her youth, Denise's attention remained focused on improving her archery skills, winning competitions and having a good time while she did so.

"I never placed parameters or limits upon myself by thinking that I was (a) better (archer) than this person or that person," stated Denise. "I wouldn't challenge myself to shoot a particular score, either. I focused instead on not only doing my best every time I shot, but also becoming the best that I could be."

With age comes wisdom, something the grown-up Parker seems to possess in a large quantity.

"I think people who set attainable goals for themselves may limit themselves without realizing it," she explained. "When a goal that was once considered extremely difficult, or even unattainable, is finally reached I think an athlete sometimes inadvertently psyches himself or herself out of (continuing to improve). The mountain has been scaled, whether by shooting a particular score or besting another competitor, and, in a way, there's nowhere else to go."

Ed Eliason, a three-time Olympian and member of the gold-medal winning U.S. Pan American men's team, provided an an example of how Denise motivated herself to excel. "She sets no limitations for herself," said Eliason. "She'll ask, 'What do you think I should (shoot) at 50 meters?' I'll say, 'Do 325 (score) or 330,' and she'll do it."

Until Denise struck Pan American gold, her life elsewhere had remained fairly normal, despite hours of daily practice, occasional distant coaching sessions and numerous trips to competitions.

A Teenage Archer's Quest for Olympic Glory

She remained a fun-loving teenager, who was close to her parents, had plenty of friends, a wide array of interests and a remarkable talent. The pressures that compelled her to excel came mostly from within. She wanted to be the best at everything, and despite schoolwork, practice, competition and travel she continued to strive toward that goal.

Dark clouds, however, were massing in the distance and started moving in her direction.

Media Pressure

Denise's return home, after the Pan Am Games, was unlike any homecoming she'd ever had before. Family, friends, neighbors, schoolmates and even residents of surrounding areas, much of

Media coverage started at an early age. Here I am being interviewed by Steve Cyphers, who went on to be a correspondent for ESPN.

One of my first interviews with local reporter Reece Stein of the Utah Summer Games.

Utah in fact, now regarded her as almost a conquering hero, which the girl found somewhat inexplicable as well as more than a little disconcerting.

"My life changed, totally," Denise said. "Winning the gold medal (at the Pan Am Games) had made me almost a household

A Teenage Archer's Quest for Olympic Glory

name in Salt Lake City and much of Utah."

Many people crave celebrity. Most, however, aren't so willing to compromise their sense of privacy to obtain it, especially if they're reserved or shy, both adjectives her friends readily used to describe the girl. But she was now recognized everywhere she went. People would approach to talk as though they were her long, lost friends. Kids she'd never met would say, 'Oh, you're that archer,' while schoolmates would often whisper to each other when they passed in the hall. Denise, like most 13-year-olds, despised the constant

My mom and me getting "wired" for a Disney interview.

Denise Parker

Here I am on the cover of Parade magazine, January 24, 1988; noted freelance writer Dotson Rader came to South Jordan and conducted the interview.

attention. She hated being on display for all the world to see.

"I just wanted to be 13 and one of the gang like I'd always been" Denise remembers thinking.

Yet everyone in her neighborhood was excited, even Denise's playmates and friends. She was just 13, and yet somehow, some

A Teenage Archer's Quest for Olympic Glory

way she'd become the best female archer in the country. She was good one day, the best on the next, and it seemed like she'd done it almost overnight. A definite buzz arose about her chances of accomplishing what once had seemed an impossibility: becoming the country's youngest Olympic archer in history.

The Pan Am Games represented a breakout on the national level. Denise was suddenly besieged by media requests for personal appearances and interviews. Representatives from *Parade, Sports Illustrated, The New York Times* and nearly every other major magazine as well as many newspapers flooded the Parker family's phone lines as reporters and booking agents jockeyed for a chance to interview the young sports star.

"We didn't hire an agent," Denise recalled. "My mother took the calls and booked the interviews. Every single day it seemed we'd get additional requests for interviews, talk show appearances and photo shoots, but I hated it. My mother would tell me a particular magazine would be there the next week and I'd whine, Why do I have to do that? Some people even asked me to give talks before audiences, another thing I didn't enjoy doing at the time."

One incident remains firmly embedded in her memory. "I was home alone when someone called from the Johnny Carson *(Tonight Show)* show called. When I answered, a lady said she wanted to book me on the show. I asked her when, checked the appointment calendar and then replied, 'I'm going hunting that week.'"

"The lady laughed. 'Why don't you have your mother call me when she gets home,' she responded.

"My mother just about flipped out when she heard what I'd done," Denise continued. Valerie, of course, knew that Johnny Carson was one of the most beloved TV personalities of the past

59

50 years, and his show consistently scored huge ratings. She called back and told Carson's representative that Denise would appear, but requested a date change so the family could still go hunting as planned.

Denise, unfortunately, cut her finger so severely, while on the hunting trip, that the wound required stitches. Her *Tonight Show* appearance had to be rescheduled yet again since Carson wanted Denise to demonstrate her skill for his audience. "My finger was pretty bad," Denise said. "I couldn't shoot at all for a while."

When she finally appeared on Carson's Los Angeles -based nighttime talk show, the two bantered together like old friends. "We discussed archery, school and boys. I told Johnny, I like two boys right now but both are mad at me. What should I do?"

The quick-witted Carson, who'd been a party to several messy and highly public divorces, immediately shot back, "I don't know if you're asking the right person," he quipped.

Carson realized that while most of the world had heard about the young archery phenomenon, few had actually seen her shoot. To remedy that his staff had set up a number of 'targets' for Denise to shoot at. Denise's first arrow drilled an ordinary archery target. The girl then shot out two balloons, a vase, and two eggs and demolished a Lifesaver mint. At one point during the exhibition, Denise shot a buzzing alarm clock.

"Wouldn't you love to wake up in the morning and do that when it goes off?" said Carson after watching his guest terminate the clock.

"Johnny Carson was great," Denise said. "I think I enjoyed him more than anyone else I met during those years. He was so funny and he spoke with me like he'd known me for years. He didn't talk down to me, like some people had a tendency to do. Plus, I had a lot of fun in the Green Room" (where guests waited before being summoned onto The *Tonight Show's* stage).

Celebrity interviewer Dotson Rader also came calling. Rader flew out from New York on assignment for *Parade Magazine,* the weekly news supplement that's included with most major U.S. Sunday or weekend newspapers.

"Rural Utah had never seen anyone quite like Dotson Rader," Denise recalled. "Utah was laid back, and super-conservative and South Jordan was still mostly farmland. In rushed Dotson, so flamboyant and big city. I'm still not sure he quite knew what to make of my family and our hunting, although he later wrote a wonderful article."

That article garnered the prestigious *Parade* cover for the teenager, a place of honor usually reserved for celebrities or politicians of the highest order. Numerous photos of Denise and her family accompanied Rader's article, which spawned even more interest in the girl.

In the article, Rader, who had covered quite a wide variety of questions when researching his article, had also inquired about the boys and boyfriends.

"I told Mr. Rader that my dream guy was Kirk Cameron, the star of *Growing Pains* (a popular TV show of the late 1980s)," said Denise. Like many 13-year-olds, Denise had posters of Kirk all over her room, and told Rader so. Rader, naturally, reported the teenager's TV star crush in his article, although Denise didn't think much about it at the time.

A few days later, Denise once more was home alone when the phone rang.

"Is this Denise Parker?" a voice inquired, after she'd answered. Denise replied that it was.

"This is Kirk Cameron," the voice responded.

Sure it is, Denise thought to herself, sensing that she was about to be sucked into a joke.

The caller must have sensed her hesitation because he said, "You don't believe me, do you?"

"No, I don't," Denise admitted.

"What if I send you an autographed—by me—copy of Parade? Would you believe me then?"

"Maybe," she said.

After hanging up the phone, Denise had an epiphany. "Maybe that really *was* Kirk Cameron," I suddenly thought. "But I had no way of calling him back" (since this occurred before the availability of Caller ID and Call Return telephone services).

"A week later an envelope addressed to me arrived in the mail, with a television studio listed as the return address" Denise continued. "Sure enough, folded inside was a copy of the *Parade* article, signed by Kirk Cameron." Cameron never called back even though Denise would have believed him the next time.

The Pressure Cooker

Along with the incessant media pressure, which was distracting enough, Denise now detected attitude changes in some of the people closest to her, including her father and Tim Strickland, one of her coaches.

As she practiced with Strickland following the Pan Am Games, Denise realized that she wasn't having nearly as much fun as she'd had before her big win. As expectations ratcheted skyward, the intensity level of those instructing her—even at practice—soared.

That pressure came in different ways, such as not being permitted to quit practicing once she became tired, or shooting a particular score or a certain number of arrows, like it or not, until she was finally dismissed from the practice session.

Strickland, however, remained an excellent mentor, especially about the mental aspects of dealing with competitive pressures. "Tim reinforced in me the importance of remaining calm at all times, even when the pressure became overwhelming."

Strickland, to his credit, never reacted in a negative fashion when his star student didn't shoot up to expectations, according to Denise. Neither did he dwell on her subpar performances.

Strickland knew exactly what Denise was going through since he himself had been a competitive archer as well as an archery coach. Strickland understood that archers, like other top athletes, must sometimes work through periods when their accuracy is simply off, for whatever reason. When Denise suffered such a decline, during this period, Strickland helped the teenager understand how athletes occasionally seem to take a step backward before they're able to take the two steps forward that will lead to an even higher competitive plane.

Tim Strickland remained a good choice on a number of levels, yet the coach-student dynamic, Denise felt, had definitely shifted. The shift affected the archer, yet she rather astutely understood the real truth of her situation: Strickland wasn't there to be her buddy, but to improve her shooting.

Denise felt she could deal with the subtle changes that had affected her relationship with Strickland. Dealing with those that had affected her primary coach, the one with whom she practiced every day, proved much tougher to bear.

Family Pressures

"After I'd won the Pan Am Games and the hype began in earnest, things started changing between my dad and me," said Denise, hesitantly. She's now an adult, but still rather reluctant to discuss a period still painful to recall.

"I know my dad never stopped wanting me to do my best," she explained. "But after the Pan Am Games, the desire for me to do well increased. It became more personal. I really think it somehow became more about him."

Earl Parker knew from the moment he'd first recognized his daughter's intensity, determination and talent, that he might have a budding champion on his hands. Earl may have thought, in the way of dads everywhere, that the job of nourishing the champion-that-might-be within his child was one only he could do best. He was right, in a way, along with all the other fathers and mothers of profoundly talented children. No one wants their children to do as well, and no one knows their kids as well as their own parents.

And yet the terms 'stage mother' or 'hockey dad' are freighted with negative connotations that come not from parents loving their children too much, but from becoming such strict taskmasters, in their desire to do the best for their kids, that they then lose sight of what's important. Such as, that their youngsters are still KIDS and shouldn't be forced to grow up too quickly, and that youngsters want and need their parents' love and approval more than anything in the world, even a champion's crown, worldwide recognition and untold riches.

Earl Parker never wavered in his love of his daughter, and yet his daughter didn't know that. The best—or nearly best—archer in the U.S. was just entering her teenaged years, a time of raging hormones. As anyone who still remembers being a teenager can attest, those hormones can send even a level-headed youngster plunging into a morass of doubt, fear and uncertainty. More than ever before, teens require their parents' love and understanding during puberty. Even the kid with the world's brightest future just ahead of her, if only she'd knuckle down and under and do exactly as she was told . . .

And therein lay the problem. Earl loved Denise. And Denise wanted to please her father. As time passed, however, tension slowly increased until the Parkers could be compared to two locomotives on the same track, but rushing toward one another from opposite directions. Under those circumstances a crash is all but inevitable.

"If I shot poorly that day, dad would be all night on the phone searching for an immediate 'fix' for my problem," explained Denise. "He was trying to help me, but I was 13 and I didn't see it that way.

"I only knew he'd been my buddy, and now everything was suddenly all business. He'd get upset with me, and that would make me upset. The atmosphere at home began to feel like 24 hours of training without let-up. After a poor practice session I'd say I wanted to go home, but he wouldn't let me. We started fighting all the time. Even at dinner he'd want to talk about what I'd done wrong at practice."

Denise admitted that sometimes it felt like a lot to bear, but that feeling never lasted long. "If my dad hadn't been there for me, pushing me always to do my best, I'd never have been as successful as I was," she stated.

Denise, who's now a parent herself, can look back upon that time with empathy for her father. She can better understand what he wanted to accomplish and why. "Fathers, I think, get overly involved with their daughters because they feel that only they can help them and protect them," she mused. "And when their daughters succeed, I think fathers more readily (bask) in their daughters' success (as belonging in some ways to them as well), and that makes fathers feel good in return.

Denise Parker

"My Mom was my savior during this time," said Denise. "No matter what may have happened, I always knew she'd still love me. I could stop shooting or quit archery completely, but life would go on as it had before. I can honestly say her love for me was never based on how I was shooting that day."

"I was always worried, however, that my dad would love me only if I won," she admitted.

To her credit, Denise realizes that her father had inadvertently put himself in a position with which he was unfamiliar. He wanted Denise to excel, but she'd now excelled beyond even his considerable imaginings. What should he do now with a kid so talented she was exceeding beyond all expectation? He must have wondered. Earl Parker, Denise now understands, was probably dealing with issues of his own that were as taxing to him as were Denise's to her.

The 13-year-old Denise, even the 17-year-old Denise, didn't know this or even try to consider its possibility, but then how many teenagers in similar situations would?

Denise's father next arranged for her to meet with Keith Henschen, a sports psychologist on staff at the University of Utah. Henschen was charged with helping Denise develop a thorough psychological approach to archery as a way of further improving her shooting.

Henschen spent a lot of time helping Denise grasp the concept of visualization as it applies to sport. The girl began to practice at home, in her bedroom even, by visualizing a perfect 10—bullseye—shot and then trying to keep that vision in her mind. By visualizing 10s, when such a shot appeared in real life Denise would recognize it immediately and seize that moment to make the shot.

"Visualization is all about recognizing a good shot before you take it," Denise explained.

Henschen also worked to improve the archer's focus or concentration, one of the most important elements in the sport. Total concentration on the task at hand is extremely difficult, and even more so if you're a young teenaged girl, so Henschen next developed concentration exercises that used the same techniques that Denise had previously applied during visualization.

'Recognizing a good shot' may sound like child's play to those who have have never shot bow or gun. Yet doing exactly that forms the very basis of both accuracy and consistency. A small thing, perhaps, and yet championships are won by those who pay attention to the smallest details.

Pressure and Friends

A girl of 13 is on the cusp of womanhood. Her body is changing, and so is the place she occupies in the world. Boys and men will never look at her again in quite the same way as they did a year or two earlier. That in itself can be disconcerting to a youngster.

Most teenagers, as they move toward adulthood, rely on friends for support. Teenage girls share their hopes, their fears, their everyday experiences almost everywhere they congregate—at school, the mall, the movies and during overnights at each others' homes.

Imagine, however, what that would be like if the spotlight were on you, if only briefly. Kids at school start recognizing you, many of them can be heard whispering, 'That's the archer,' or 'She was on the cover of *Parade*.'

Denise never wanted to stand out from the crowd. Like all 13-year-olds, she wanted to be like everyone else and would have done anything to fit in.

Hearing the remarks and noticing the glances, both covert and blatant, only caused the teenager to retreat further into the shell she'd started building around her. She became shyer and more introverted when among people she didn't know. Her further withdrawal, into archery as well as her own tight-knit circle of friends, was totally misunderstood. People started commenting that Denise was stuck up or conceited when she was simply somewhat anxious and shy.

Such underhanded statements would have bothered her even more than they did had it not been for her network of friends. She lived for the moments she could spend time or play games with them, the way she'd once occupied almost every day of the year. She now traveled so much, especially in summer, that she was unable to be involved in many activities that other kids take for granted. Summer camps, dances, hanging out—Denise missed almost everything. She remained in the thick of things whenever school was in session, but in summer, Denise felt like something of an outcast, despite having friends both at school and in archery. ∎

Chapter 7
Qualifying for the Olympics

The Road to Seoul

After the victory at the Pan Am Games, Denise was asked what plans she had for the future.

"I hope to be competitive with the best in the world by the Olympics," Denise replied. "But if I went to the Olympics and lost, it wouldn't make me quit. Just being there means you're good, and that would be satisfaction enough."

Denise could get plenty of satisfaction simply from what she'd accomplished in 1987. She was named the National Archery Association's Female Athlete of the Year and honored by the U.S. Olympic Committee as Woman Archer of the Year. A resolution had been passed in her honor by the Utah State Senate that wished her success in achieving her Olympic goals. She met with the Honorable Norm Bangerter, Utah's governor, then traveled to Washington, D. C., to meet Utah Senator Orrin Hatch and President Ronald Reagan as part of the Women in Sports Day celebration.

The presidential meeting was especially memorable because it took place in the Oval Office. The archer and the leader of the free world clicked immediately, and Denise recalls President Reagan with special fondness.

"I liked him immediately," she said. "He seemed so warm, like he was genuinely interested in me, what I'd done and what I was trying to do."

Denise Parker

Denise and President Ronald Reagan

Denise had setbacks, too. She was young enough to cry when her score failed to meet personal expectations. One poor shot during that year's Olympic Trials Festival sent her standing plummeting in the competition from second to eighth. Denise buckled down, made the rest of her shots count and finished fourth, not as high as she'd hoped but not as poorly as she'd feared during a few anxious moments.

She'd also attended another JOAD camp and won the follow-up

National JOAD Championships competition. She repeated as National Junior Indoor Champion, and was the youngest competitor named to the U. S. National Junior Olympic Elite Team. She went to Japan as a representative of both the U. S. and her sport and appeared on a national TV show called *Super Kids of the World*.

And she'd soon be entering eighth grade.

Life so far had been pretty good. Her journey to the upper echelons of her sport had been nothing less than meteoric. The pressures had increased as well, but with the help of parents, coaches and teachers she'd handled them deftly and gracefully.

No one early on could have anticipated such an unbelievable level of success, and yet success had its downsides: the changing attitudes of coach and father, plus external pressures that never seemed to let up. The downside that most worried the Parkers, at

Me learning to eat with chopsticks in Japan. This is how I spent my summer vacations.

this juncture in their daughter's career, was the most formidable they'd yet faced: how to pay for the many expenses that were mounting up at an increasing pace?

The Money Issue

Young competitors on the local level rarely worry much about money. But once Denise's skill level had advanced beyond the capabilities of local instructors, when travel to distant states and countries—sometimes with extended stays—became increasingly necessary and with no let-up in sight, the family's financial situation began to teeter on the brink of precarious.

The family's savings had become seriously depleted during her years of competition. Her parents had been well aware, as Denise began her climb, that financial support was necessary and that the help their daughter required wouldn't come cheaply, yet they'd willingly paid whatever was needed to keep Denise advancing to the next level. With the Olympic summit finally in their sight, they reluctantly acknowledged that continuing to fund their daughter's odyssey could be a financial hardship. In that they weren't much different from most families of the American middle class, either then or now.

And the girl's serious Olympic training had yet to begin.

The Parkers knew that the world's finest athletes can never simply rest on their laurels, not when the Olympics are slightly more than a year away. Additional coaching is a must, even for the most talented athletes. The ideal situation—what every Olympian's coach strives to achieve—to have his athlete's performance peak both during qualifying and when competing in the Games. Wanting that to happen and having it happen, however, are two very different things.

The expenses associated with competing don't cease suddenly when one becomes a member of a country's Olympic team. Continued competition is important. It provides needed experience and practice for athletes intent on steeling their nerves and steadying their eyes. Competitions are held in all kinds of weather—high wind, searing heat and even rain, providing archers with opportunities to see how well they perform, and what adjustments must be made if an important competition takes place during adverse conditions. Only by competing will an archer be able to fully refine the the elements of concentration required of anyone who must perform before the world's largest audience, one comprised of fans, family, friends, teammates, coaches, other Olympians and the media.

To maintain her competitive edge Denise, her father and Tim Strickland decided that the teenager should participate in three archery meets before the mid-June Olympic Trials, and an additional two competitions afterwards. The schedule would be arduous, and include trips to Colorado, Virginia, Colorado, Ohio, Florida and back to Ohio.

The Parkers also began to worry that with Denise now competing seriously during the school year for the first time the girl's 3.7 grade point average might suffer. Grades were a major consideration because, in less than four years, Denise would be taking her college placement tests. Good grades were imperative if she hoped to be accepted by a college of her choice. Denise's education was such an important consideration the family even considered hiring a tutor to aid Denise while she was traveling although it never became necessary to do so.

Before 1992, competitors who aspired to become Olympians were not allowed to accept money for winning competitions or for endorsing products connected to their sports. To do so would result in the loss of an athlete's amateur status, and at the time, only amateurs were allowed to compete in the Olympics.

In 1992, however, this changed when professional basketball players were invited to compete as members of the U. S. team. Many other Olympians are now highly-paid professionals, including both men's and women's basketball, softball, baseball, track and field and tennis players.

In 1988, however, none of the competitors had much money. Denise wasn't old enough to work to earn money for training or travel for her coach, but even athletes old enough to get a job rarely did because training took up so much of their time. That was especially true if the athlete was in college, which many of them were.

The money crunch preyed most on Denise's parents' minds. They'd supported her, emotionally and financially, during her improbable venture to the very apex of her sport. Now that she was so close to attaining what she'd set out to accomplish, would it be lack of money—and not ability—that would shatter their dreams?

Certainly this was the last thing Jim Easton, of Easton Aluminum wanted. He stepped up to add much needed financial support. Easton supplied equipment to Denise and donated money to help cover her and her coach Tim Strickland's travel expenses. This relieved much of the direct expenses associated with competition and travel for Denise but there were still the issue of her parents travel (Denise was still only 13) along with other expenses associated with training which were borne by the Parkers.

A Solution

That winter, with the 1988 Winter Olympics ready to get underway in Calgary, Alberta, Ann Dawson, a Parker friend and South Jordan neighbor, knew it was time to get busy. Dawson had asked Valerie Parker, some months earlier, to let her know if the family ever needed help of any kind. Dawson suggested a community fund-raiser, if money were to become a problem, which it had. Dawson would be the ramrod of the affair, an Italian spaghetti dinner to be held in the local elementary school.

Neighbor helping neighbor has always been the Utah way. Community spirit—helping out when needed—now entered the picture, and it couldn't have come at a more welcome time.

Ann Dawson started contacting people to explain about the fundraiser and why it was necessary. Once people became aware of the problems facing the Parkers, help seemed to come from all quarters. Local newspapers helped publicize the event at no cost by running articles, notices and advertisements. Businesses donated food and supplies for what was hoped would be a substantial turnout. One business donated the amount needed to rent Welby Elementary School's cafeteria for the evening. An individual donor provided drinks for the expected crowd.

On the day of the event, so many people were attempting to get served (during one memorable moment) that workers couldn't cook, drain and dish out spaghetti fast enough to keep up. While the patient crowd waited for dinner, Denise entertained them with a demonstration of her archery skills. The attendees soon felt pretty good about helping Denise go to the Olympics. The teenager shot 27 arrows, all of them bulls-eyes. By the end of the evening more than $4,500 had been raised. Other fund-raising activities followed, including an electronic tag game and a dance at which a

D.J. spun records. Contributors could donate money directly into a bank account, set up in Denise's name by her father's employer, The Newspaper Agency, and administered by The National Archery Association.

Denise also starred in a television commercial touting a low-interest MasterCard (credit card). Payment for Denise's 6 1/2 hours of on-camera work and permission to use her image in their campaign also came as a payment into the account. Other company promotions followed, each of them adding something to the total, which finally relieved much of the pressure on the Parkers.

Taking Care of Business

Pressure of other sorts, however, continued to build on their daughter from other directions.

A New York television crew traveled to South Jordan to film Denise for a one-hour Disney Channel documentary about aspiring young Olympians. The crew tagged along with her everywhere as they tried to get enough footage to depict a representative slice of her life. Filming her in training at home was bad enough, but they also tagged along when she competed in the National Archery Association Indoor Regional/National competition in Colorado Springs, Colorado, where she once more set records in both junior and women's divisions.

The camera became a particular embarrassment to the girl after they traipsed into her school to film candid shots of the girl interacting with eighth-grade classmates. The crew, amazingly, seemed unable to understand why Denise did her best to avoid them. Denise, however, was always in a state of dread when she was with her friends or neighbors while the media were hovering nearby.

A Teenage Archer's Quest for Olympic Glory

Along with embarrassment, came incredible opportunities. So many, that the Parkers could scarcely fit them into Denise's increasingly hectic schedule. Denise, now 14, who'd just won the Atlantic City (New Jersey) Archery Classic over Melanie Skillman 1,126 to 1,120, barely had time to savor the victory before she was flying enroute to Peking, the capitol of China. There she and seven other U. S. archers competed in the three-day Chinese National Archery Competition where Denise finished fifth. The U. S. archers were also treated to a deluxe tour of China, an experience beyond the means of most of the rest of the world.

The packed-to-overflowing archery schedule eventually caused Denise to drop all other recreational sports. She tried for a time to shoe-horn softball into her training regimen but was unable to, thanks to the time crunch. Where once she'd enjoyed many different sports and activities, the scope of her life seemed to be narrowing until she only had room for archery. The other fun things she'd once enjoyed had started to fade away under the intense glare of the spotlight.

Training meant shooting about 150–200 arrows a day. In addition to daily archery practice, Denise was running three or four miles several days each week, training with free weights and on machines, in a never-ending quest to improve strength and stamina. Each shot with a bow required the teenager to pull back on the bow-string as the limbs flexed into position and then hold the 30 pounds of stored energy, now coiled within the bow, until it was released. Shooting just 100 arrows was the equivalent of pulling and holding, until the string's release, about 3,000 pounds—a ton and a half—of cumulative weight.

"Denise is mentally tough," Strickland pointed out. "And in my opinion, 80-percent of the preparation (for a competition) is mental.

"In years past (a coach) would teach people to shoot and then hope they'd win a gold medal," he continued. "That (attitude) was a bunch of garbage because such a big part of archery is mental. Other countries have made huge advances in (Olympic competitors') mental preparation. We (in the U. S.) have to play their game if we want to catch up."

This innate mental toughness may help explain why the youngster was able to put so much distance, so quickly, between herself and older, more experienced archers with Olympic aspirations. (The average age of an Olympian is between 20 and 30 years old).

The Trials

Denise's schedule had become so demanding that the family decided to allow her to start summer vacation three weeks before school formally ended that year. With eighth grade now but a memory, the girl got the present off to a resounding start by becoming the first female archer in history to shoot 1,300 in a FITA—Federation of International Target Archers—round. She scored 1,301 out of a possible 1,440 as she, in spectacular fashion, won the Championship of the Americas trials in Harrisonburg, Virginia.

However grand the accomplishment, Denise knew it would fade from mind the moment she stepped up to the firing line at the Olympic Trials. What once had seemed a lifetime away would begin in less than a month, on June 15, 1988, and conclude June 18.

In previous years, competitors had to qualify in each of several preliminary steps before the team's members were decided upon. This time, however, those archers who finished with the three top scores, in the men's competition and in the women's, would make the team. That year the trials were held at Miami

University of Ohio, in Oxford. On each of four days, aspiring Olympians must shoot two competitive rounds, men against men and women against women. At the conclusion of the trials the world would know who would represent the U. S. during the Seoul Olympics.

With the trials just two weeks distant, Denise suffered an inflamed tendon, or tendonitis, in her left, or drawing shoulder. This was most likely caused by the constant pressure to shoot a greater bow weight combined with over-working the muscles.

The tendonitis was painful, but waiting four more years before trying out again would be more unbearable. She'd worked too hard to cave in to a physical malady. She would give the trials a go, tendonitis or not. Her mind was made up, perhaps because both Tim Strickland and sports psychologist Keith Henschen had been urging the girl to cultivate a winning attitude through mental and psychological exercises.

They'd done their jobs well. "Sometimes I'd even visualize myself on a podium with a gold medal around my neck."

"It's crucial for (Denise) to win a contest in her mind before she even goes out to shoot," Strickland added.

At the end of the first day of the trials, Denise trailed Debra Ochs by one point, 619 to 618. The teenager, who usually averaged as much as 30 points more at 60 and 70 meters, the distances shot that day, had been plagued by a flare-up of the tendonitis. It hindered her mobility which, in turn, affected the girl's usually spot-on accuracy. Pain flared when she began to draw the bow as well as near the end of her shooting motion when she had to hold at full draw, however briefly, before the release. That evening Denise was holding an ice bag against her sore left shoulder, even as she continued to downplay to the media and other bystanders the amount of pain she was feeling.

Tendonitis often becomes chronic, which means it might linger for weeks, months and even longer. Denise, however, 'toughed it out' and refused to allow the ailment to affect her performance during later rounds. By the end of the second day, Denise was in first place. The following morning, she shot her worst score of the event and finished the day in second. Denise was able to calm down and relax by Tuesday afternoon when she took over the top slot steadily increased her lead over the field.

Wind was definitely a factor during the day's competition. Shooting in wind is more difficult than during still conditions. Compensating for 'windage'—the amount to the left or right an arrow may veer off course due to wind—becomes more of a problem when winds are variable since both wind direction and speed can change in a matter of moments. Shooters often have no idea how such a wind will affect arrow flight until after they've shot. All they can do is 'guesstimate,' to the best of their knowledge, how the wind will affect the next shot and adjust their aim accordingly.

On the final day of the competition during the Grand FITA finals, (a Grand FITA for women consists of shooting nine arrows at each of four distances—30, 50, 60 and 70 meters, distances equivalent to slightly more than 90, 150, 180 and 210 feet) and with a place on the Olympic team already assured, Denise continued to dominate, despite the tendonitis. Her victory was resounding as she became the first U. S. female ever to score more than 330 points—she scored 331—of a possible 360.

Debbie Ochs, of Howell, Michigan, and Melanie Skillman, of Laureldale, Pennsylvania, finished in second and third place respectively to also make the team.

Tim Strickland was pleased. "(Denise's score) is world class," he stated. "If she shoots like that in the Olympics she'll be right up with the best."

Only recently had female archers from Korea, considered the world's finest shooters, broke 330 in Grand FITA events.

"Denise has ice water in her veins," added Budd Rose, one of the teenager's first archery instructor. "She's got to have, to shoot like that."

"Denise is a good kid who's shooting incredibly well," added Luann Ryon. "It's what archery needs—new blood. She's got a good head, and she's not afraid."

The men's Olympic archery team had also been decided upon and included Jay Barrs, of Mesa, Arizona, Darrell Pace, of Hamilton, Ohio, and Rick McKinney, of Gilbert, Arizona. Barrs finished in first, well ahead of Pace who'd earned Olympic gold at both the 1976 and 1984 Games. McKinney, the 1984 men's silver medalist, held off Ed Eliason, 50, at the time.

"We've got the three best shooters in the world going (to Seoul)," McKinney stated, of the U. S. men's archery team. "The way Jay (Barrs) is shooting he's a definite gold-medal possibility."

McKinney wasn't merely expressing his opinion, but that of much of the world: the talent on the U. S. men's team was exceptional. Expectations for the women's archery team were less high. Historically, the women's archery powerhouse teams were fielded by Korea, Russia, and China.

The 1988 Olympic Summer Games marked the first time archers would vie not only for individual medals, but for team medals as well. Each member of the three top-scoring teams also would win medals.

Knowing that they had an increased chance of winning a medal during the Games came as welcome news to Denise. Less welcome was the sudden realization that Trena King and Luann Ryon, her two mentors and friends, had failed to make the team.

Denise Parker

The scoreboard at the Olympic Trails in 1988.

Expectations

The moment Denise became a *bona fide* member of the 1988 U. S. Olympic Archery Team everything changed. No longer must she worry about making the team, she'd done so.

Denise already knew and liked Sheri Rhodes, coach of the U. S. women's archery team, since she'd spent time with Rhodes and Rick McKinney before she competed in the Pan American trials.

Her gradually maturing physique would help her blend in as well as compete more as an equal. At the Pan Am Games she'd been 4-foot-11 and weighed 89 pounds. She now stood 5-foot-3 and weighed 105-pounds.

She'd miss the the first few weeks of school, where she'd now be a ninth grader, because of the Olympics and yet no one seemed worried since she'd continued to maintain her grade point average. Her unusual lifestyle—travel to far-flung locales, exposure to diverse cultures and competition in myriad events with people much older than her—had provided Denise with the wisdom,

A Teenage Archer's Quest for Olympic Glory

poise and 'street smarts' of someone ten years her senior.

The extra height and weight, augmented by muscles developed during years of working out, had also helped Denise progress to the use of a higher draw-weight bow, a 31-pound recurve 68-inches in length. Were she to have placed one end of the bow upon the ground the other would still have towered above her head. Denise's draw-weight was still somewhat less than those of other U. S. team members, but no longer was the discrepancy so glaring.

Growing Up Denise

Those who made their livings in the newly popular archery industry had become aware of subtle changes in Denise during the time she'd been competing. Expectations remained as high as ever, but now some people were boldly predicting that Denise would abandon the sport once she discovered boys and dating. One such

The 1988 Olympic Team at the Olympic Trails. Jay Barrs and I qualified in first place.

individual—Bob Rhode, of Hoyt Archery—made a rather public $100 bet with ex-U. S. National Champion Jim Pickering that by 1989 Denise would no longer be involved in archery.

Denise, by the way, made note of the bet and, on the day in question, took time off to visit Rhode personally and inform him that he owed Pickering $100.

Perhaps because Denise had been so successful, talk now began that centered on how she 'hadn't really paid her dues' because it hadn't taken her as long to work her way up through the ranks. Denise heard other talk as well, and not all of it was flattering or complimentary. Such comments hurt her deeply, especially those spoken to her in person, yet she continued to maintain an aura of professionalism as she went about her business and refused to

Melanie Skillman, me, and Debbie Ochs at the Championship of the Americas in Caracas, Venezuela.

listen or let the negative comments sink in. She had little time for such nonsense. She wouldn't get mad, she'd bide her time and then someday get even.

"All the talk just steeled my resolve," Denise commented. "Nothing inspires me more than proving someone's misconceptions."

The Team

Once Denise qualified for the U. S. archery team she was required to travel with the team to training camp, as well as to all competitions preceding the Olympics.

The 14-year-old had gone from hanging out with her parents to becoming almost an 'adopted' little sister to Trena King and Luann Ryon, her Pan Am Trials and Games buddies. She now became something of an odd woman out when she became the teammate of Deborah Ochs and Melanie Skillman.

"I didn't fit in," Denise explained. "I can't blame Deborah or Melanie, either, because the age gap was huge." Unlike Trena King and Luann Ryon, Denise's new teammates weren't as kid-oriented.

Denise couldn't have gone as far as she had without being adaptable. She started tagging along with members of the men's team and quickly became one of their favorite people because of her youth, fun-loving attitude and love of sports.

"Jay Barrs was my buddy," Denise recalled, of the top-ranked American male archer. "He was in college, so he wasn't too much older than me. He could be so goofy. He was always laughing or teasing me and when he wasn't he'd sometimes carry me around on his shoulders. We had a lot of fun."

When Denise craved competition other than archery she'd look for Barrs or Rick McKinney.

"Jay and I played basketball and tennis together," Denise said. "Rick and I ran together."

Being thrust into adult company during her formative years helped speed up the rate at which Denise matured. Competing so much meant she often was on the road where she grew accustomed to adult conversation. She also picked up the habit of swearing, particularly once she made the Olympic team.

"Steve Lieberman was the manager of the U. S. Olympic Team," said Denise. "He swore all the time, without thinking. I gave him grief about it, but then I started swearing, too. That sort of shocked the other archers and they joined in to remind Steve to clean up his language, since he was such a bad influence on me."

The 1988 Olympics in Seoul, Korea, would be the most important event of Denise's life and yet she had little time to think about how she'd actually do there. She was kept busy competing in the Junior Olympic Nationals, in Florida, and the Championship of the Americas, in Caracas, Venezuela, in which she competed as a member of the U. S. Olympic team.

The rest of the time the teenager was discovering how becoming an Olympian, one of the most elite athletes in the world, would change her life in ways both large and small. ∎

Chapter 8
The Olympic Atmosphere

Preparations

Denise's world dissolved into a whirlwind of Olympics-related activities. The media hype that preceded her participation in the Olympic Trials added to TV and print coverage during and after the trials had almost guaranteed the anointing of the young Utahan as America's Sweetheart during the Seoul games.

Someone other than Denise might have felt her head turned by the attention being devoted to passionate discussion of the young archer's chances in Seoul.

Not Denise, however; her feet remained planted solidly on *terra firma*.

"I'm trying to be realistic," Denise said, to one reporter at the time. "For me to win the gold medal, I'd have to shoot what for me would be an unbelievable score."

The young archer knew that although she might be one of America's best archers, she was far from being one of the world's best female archers. Had someone asked who that might be, Denise together with much of the archery world, probably, would have replied, "Kim Su Nyung." Korea's Nyung, 17, that January had scored a world-record 1,338 points during Asia Cup competition, 37 points over Denise's top score.

As superb an archer as Denise may have been, once she was spotlighted upon the world's stage she would be merely one of a host of contenders hotly pursuing the title that implicitly belongs to the reigning Olympic champion: 'world's best.' Those contenders included more than 30 South Korean women who'd shot 1,300 or more, the U.S.S.R.'s Ludmila Arzhannikova, who consistently scored over 1,300, and Ma Xiagjun, of China, the current world champion. Qualifying for the Olympics, Denise and her coaches had always understood, would be far easier than winning or even earning a medal.

Yet no matter how difficult an Olympic win might have seemed, Denise wanted to live up to her own expectations of success. She remembered Debi Thomas, the popular black U.S. figure skater who'd been widely expected to win the gold, but settled for silver, and resolved not to settle for anything other than her best. Her goal had been simply to make the Olympics, and while her expectations remained high, she continued to be a realist. "I know how tough it will be to win a medal," she said.

"I don't know if I can beat them (the other competitors)," she continued. "But I can shoot with them. (And) the better the competition, the better I usually do.

"People say I've got plenty of time; that I can return in 1992 and for 20 years after that. Maybe I will, but there's no guarantee.

"I want to take my best shot now and see what happens," she concluded.

Upping the Ante

After the Trials, Denise took off a month from competition to rest her sore shoulder. Several times a week the teenager received ultrasound treatments for her shoulder from a physical therapist. She also did therapeutic exercises, which were boring perhaps, but also necessary.

Each day during the rehabilitation period Denise continued to 'shoot' arrows, just not real ones. She instead shot imaginary arrows, thanks to the visualization techniques she'd learned. She also visualized improving her release of the bow-string, and when she started shooting again for real she was pleased to discover that her release was smoother, more fluid and better than ever before, and proved to her own satisfaction, once and for all, the value of the process.

She also began to incorporate other aspects of sports psychology into her training schedule. The Parkers had always visited Keith Henschen as a family, which Denise approved of since everyone would then be familiar with the goals set for her and exercises suggested by the psychologist.

Those goals included further developing her powers of concentration as well as the efficient use of relaxation techniques to use during the stress of Olympic competition. To those ends Henschen taught Denise to tense, then relax, each muscle in her body. He instructed her to wear headphones so she could listen to the radio as she shot. He suggested that she listen to her heartbeat or read a book while she also listened to music between shots to help her relax.

Henschen would often instruct Denise to read one or two pages of a book while her parents discussed Denise during a normal conversation. He wanted to be certain that if the girl wanted to listen she'd be able to hear every word.

The point of the exercise was to make Denise focus or concentrate on reading the book to the exclusion of all else, even distracting personal information she wanted to hear and could have heard had she simply stopped concentrating on the text before her eyes. Everyone would know if she'd suffered a lapse in concentration, however, since after ten minutes she would be requested to tell the others what she'd just read.

Henschen subjected Denise to such ordeals for good reasons; namely, as preparation for dealing with the pressure of performing in front of an audience of perhaps 100 million people as well as banks of cameras. If the teenager could successfully tune out her parents' conversations, she would be able to ignore distractions at the Games.

Being able to relax at will, despite external pressure, was also of crucial importance. Henschen familiarized her with breathing exercises devised to relieve excess muscle tension that might negatively impact performance.

Henschen had already helped Denise create a 'happiness room,' the safe place to which she could withdraw, in her imagination, to visualize an upcoming meet. Denise, who had an active imagination anyway, learned to retreat to the imaginary haven before a competition. "There's stairs leading up to it and these big doors you go through," she said, at the time. "It has brown wall-to-wall carpet, a king-sized waterbed (after all it was the 80s), stereo, a big-screen TV and VCR, posters of Tom Cruise and Kirk Cameron and a fireplace that's always blazing. That's where I go when a meet's coming up. I drive up to it in a Porsche, go inside, lie down on the bed and watch myself shooting perfect arrows. When I finally get to the tournament, everything seems familiar."

Tim Strickland approved of Henschen's exercises, but he never wavered in his belief that his star student would withstand whatever the Olympics had in store for her.

"Denise already has experienced a lot of pressure, but still she excels," Strickland stated. "That's the mark of a born winner."

More Of Everything

Each passing day brought more good news. Easton agreed to pay Tim Strickland's fare to the Olympics, Earl's employer, the Newspaper Agency, agreed to pay for his airfare, and a major Olympic sponsor, offered a Friends and Family airfare savings promotion. The fare reduction meant covering Valerie Parker's travel expenses to Seoul would no longer be a problem.

During down time, Denise starred in a TV commercial for Crest toothpaste. She was paid residuals into her trust fund each time the commercial ran on TV.

"I'd never made much money, so the $10,000 or $15,000 I made from the commercial seemed like a lot."

In 1987, the Utah legislature lowered the state's legal hunting age from 16 to 14. Denise finally was old enough to go bowhunting.

She promptly put her first hunting license to use when she shot and killed, with a single arrow, a two-point (on one antler; four points overall) mule deer buck she'd spotted a few miles from camp. Bowhunting isn't easy. Her parents, for example, had bowhunted for seven years without tagging a buck. Yet their precocious youngster had gone out and bagged one in less than an hour.

The next year she followed her first bow-hunting feat with another by downing a seven-point buck.

Some later would have the *chutzpah* to term Denise's bowhunting success 'beginner's luck.'

"It was skill," Denise stated as she laughed, in no uncertain terms.

On Her Way

Denise's friends threw her a great going away party on the eve of her departure from Salt Lake City.

The next day she boarded her plane before a throng of fans

and admirers who wanted to wish their Olympian well in Seoul.

She was almost there, Denise thought when she reported to Team Processing where athletes were given physical exams to determine if they were healthy enough to leave the country, and received their credentials.

Ever since Palestinian extremists slaughtered twelve Israelis in Olympic Village during the 1972 Munich Games, athletes who needed access to various Olympic venues were required to have the proper credentials at all times. Credentials provided another layer of security for the athletes' overall protection.

Denise wasn't just the youngest archer on the U.S. archery team; she was the youngest of all the 639 athletes representing the U.S. in all Olympic disciplines. Only Marjorie Jestring, who was 13 years and nine months old when she won gold in women's Springboard Diving during the 1936 Olympics, had been younger than the South Jordan teen.

The teenager was wide-eyed at Team Processing merely from spotting so many of America's premier athletes at the same time. But what really made her giddy with excitement was learning that team sponsors had filled a huge room with all types of clothing and gear that was free to athletes.

"Cameras, watches and lots of clothes, just the coolest things," Denise recently exclaimed, her voice still resembling a 14-year-old's. "We were given two or three big travel bags apiece, several jackets, including those made of leather, sweats, raingear, pants and shoes."

Denise explained that the athletes would push a large grocery basket from table to table throughout the room and could pick out anything that caught their fancy. At each table someone would help the athletes get the proper sizes. Denise was astounded by everything she got; so much, in fact, she wouldn't need to pack any of her old belongings for the trip to Seoul.

Denise was astounded by all that she received that day, and called it 'one of the most memorable moments of my life.'

Before competing in Seoul, the team traveled to Tokyo, Japan where they would train at one of the country's famous, state-of-the-art sports complexes.

Mizuno, a Japanese manufacturer of athletic clothing and equipment, was an Olympic sponsor in 1988 and that meant even more free clothing for the entire team.

The complex itself was designed to provide users with opportunities to participate in many different sports, including archery, tennis, basketball and grass skiing.

"It wasn't a bad life," Denise said, with wry humor. "I kept myself so busy I don't even remember missing my parents."

Under different circumstances one would have had to hog-tie Denise to keep her away from the grass-skiing slope, especially since she already was something of an expert snow skier. But Denise knew that the momentary fun she might have enjoyed would have paled in comparison to the misery she'd feel if she fell and broke an arm or a wrist.

"You put so much time and effort into making the Olympic team, the last thing any of us wanted to do was jeopardize it by doing something stupid (like grass skiing)," explained Denise.

The team worked on mental training in Japan too, with an objective of simulating the pressure of Olympic competition by imagining that each archer had made it to the final round. Imagining such pressure, however, would be difficult if one had never before competed in the Olympics, which none of the female archers had.

Seoul, South Korea

"Getting off the plane in Seoul was pure culture shock," Denise said. "I noticed all the people, the terrible traffic and the crazy driving. If a road had three lanes in each direction for traffic, then drivers would travel in a fourth lane, of their own devising, but honking the entire time. I wondered why they even painted the lanes to begin with."

Life in Olympic Village

The U. S. Archery Team would be housed in a building that resembled almost any other four-room condominium or apartment. The floor plan reminded its occupants of a college dormitory, with two people assigned to each room.

Darrell Pace, Steve Lieberman, Melanie Skillman, Rick McKinney, me and Sheri Rhodes with the 1988 Olympic mascot.

Denise roomed with Sheri Rhodes, coach of the women's team. That way Rhodes could keep an eye on the girl to be certain nothing happened to her team's youngest member. Each morning the two shared Rhodes' manicure kit as they worked on their nails. Rhodes also braided Denise's long blonde hair. When the competition got underway, braids would help prevent flyaway hairs from annoying the teenager or obscuring her vision when on the firing line.

Denise, luckily, put aside her resulting hurt feelings after *Sports Illustrated* had printed comments attributed to Rhodes before the team left for Seoul.

"Parker is not any better or worse than the rest of them (Skillman and Ochs, Denise's Olympic teammates)," Rhodes was quoted as saying. "Everybody says Parker has the best chance at a medal, but she's never been in a tournament like this. The others have, and they might do better than anyone expects."

As for security, the events of Munich, 16 years earlier, forever changed the way the Olympics would be conducted. High fences ringed Seoul's Village, while everywhere guards armed with machine guns were stationed so they could easily conduct searches of anyone who entered the area.

"I hadn't even been born yet when the Munich Games were played," Denise commented. "I knew nothing about what had happened, but it was clearly intimidating.

"I remember wondering, 'Should I be scared?' 'Why do these people have machine guns?' I couldn't understand why anyone would want to hurt the athletes. I didn't learn about Munich until after the Games were over."

The cafeteria left a lot to be desired, according to Denise who admitted that she was somewhat finicky about the food served in

Seoul. Food Services had the formidable job of providing food, like that served at home, for teams from well over 50 nations. So intent were the Koreans on preparing something for everybody that, in the Americans' case at least, nothing tasted or looked much like the foods the Koreans were trying to replicate and the Americans were accustomed to eating.

U.S. team members and coaches who'd traveled to previous Olympics, however, expected bad food so they'd packed a supply of American beef jerky, candy and granola bars that they distributed to Olympians to trade among themselves.

"If an American wants to buy something back home, they drive to a nearby convenience store and buy it," said Denise. In South Korea, she explained Olympic Village was extremely isolated, with almost no nearby grocery and convenience stores. Were an athlete to locate such a store the only recognizable American foods she might have found were Coca Cola and perhaps some candy bars.

Looking back on the experience today, Denise regrets that she was too young at the time to appreciate and take advantage of the many chances she had to taste new or different foods.

Culture Shock

Living in Olympic Village, Denise discovered, was better than the most comprehensive geography lesson imaginable. People from countries most Americans had never heard of mingled with those from countries famous to all.

"I'd find maps so I could locate countries like Bhutan that I'd never heard of but where archery is the national sport," Denise said.

Most competitors spoke English which all but eliminated problems communicating.

Me with Missy Marlow, a gymnast Olympian from Salt Lake (who shared the same sports psychologist, Keith Henshen) at the opening ceremonies

During the 1988 Games, the U. S. S. R. was still a dictatorship. Communism had yet to fall, and sports remained an area in which the Soviets excelled.

"The Soviet coach drank a tremendous amount of vodka," Denise recalled. "He never looked drunk, but if he came close you could smell the alcohol on his breath.

"I remember being at the practice range and a Soviet archer was shooting and must have done something to aggravate the coach. He got right in her face, yelled at her and continued yelling. The woman glanced away briefly, and and the coach went sort of berserk. He slapped her four times in the face. Not little slaps, either.

"That made quite an impression," she explained. "I knew at that moment what it meant to be an American. I'm not sure I'd ever

Basketball star Ann Donovan and me at the opening ceremonies of the 1988 Olympic Games.

realized it before then. Of course, that was during a different era and a different time."

Denise soon discovered that competitors from many of the world's countries were extremely poor. Most had very little but were fascinated by the girl's rather ordinary headset radio. Everyone, it seemed, wanted to trade what little they had for something from America.

Shopping

During downtime the athletes would often go to Itaewon, a large, open shopping area similar to American malls. Visiting Itaewon, however, was somewhat creepy for blonde, blue-eyed individuals like Denise. Many South Koreans were unfamiliar with fair-complexioned, blondes. Some walked right up to her and got 'in my face,' as Denise said, to touch her hair. Denise was hesitant about going alone to the shopping area and tried always to do so in the company of other Americans for security's sake.

The Americans had no problems adjusting to South Korean prices, however. Leather jackets and shoes cost next to nothing, while Reeboks and Nikes were going for a quarter of their price back home.

The Opening Ceremony

The Olympic Opening Ceremony is often what spectators, even years later, remember most. Part pomp and circumstance, part rampant nationalism and lots of sheer spectacle, no one can usually accuse those who plan the opening ceremonies of being dull or boring.

No one, that is, except some of the athletes.

Well before the ceremony is supposed to begin, participating

Denise Parker

athletes already have been waiting, sometimes for hours, in an area where they're required to line up by the country each represents. In 1988, the opening ceremony took place on an evening when the temperature was 90-degrees. The U. S. team members were miserable, since they'd been given sweaters to wear during the ceremony.

While Denise waited for the ceremony to begin she watched for her favorite athletes. She saw Carl Lewis, the track star, and then spotted women's basketball star Ann Donovan, nearly 6 feet and 8 inches tall. Denise also sought out another Salt Lake City Olympian, gymnast Missy Marlow, who was just a few years older than Denise.

When the ceremony was about to begin, with each athlete properly positioned with each team's shortest individuals lined up toward the front of the group and with the tallest in the rear, someone yelled, "Cameras on your right!" Chaos erupted, as all the athlete tried to jockey closer to the cameras so they'd be seen on TV.

"That's the first time (the importance of the moment) really hit me," Denise said. "I stepped out onto the track and into a huge stadium while thousands of people cheered. I suddenly realized, 'This was it! The Olympics. I'd made it.' I was there, representing my country, and I was filled with pride. As we walked around the track one section was cheering wildly and waving American flags and I was almost overwhelmed. This was no longer just another archery tournament. It was the Olympics, and I was there to represent everyone in the U. S., which made it very exciting and, yes, so cool!"

Denise's Olympic experience reached an early peak when she met Greg Louganis, whom she thought quite 'hot.' Louganis later admitted that he was homosexual, which broke many female hearts. Denise also met personal athletic heroines like Olympic gold medalists Jackie Joyner-Kersee, track and field, and swimming's Janet Evans.

"The Olympics are different from football, basketball and most other sports," Denise stated. "Many Olympians have just one shot at fame. It's similar to the basketball player who's told he has just a single game in which to make his mark. Basketball players, of course, play many games during their careers. But the Olympian who doesn't do well knows it will be another four years before she can try again."

Denise would know soon enough if she would succeed or fail, and whether this would be her own never-to-be-forgotten Olympic moment.

Olympic Competition

The individual archery events that year were to be conducted over a period of four consecutive days, which meant mental and physical stamina would be extremely important. These were the first Games to use the Grand FITA system of competition and scoring. Once archers had completed two days of competition, the 24 who'd shot the highest scores would move on to the elimination rounds. Each elimination round would begin with all competitors on equal footing, with a score of zero. The 24 archers would be whittled down to 18, then 12 and finally eight. Those eight would be the event's finalists.

The Grand FITA was chosen because organizers thought it would be more visually exciting than previous individual archery competitions had been. For the first time, a TV audience would watch archers competing in a sudden elimination format against other archers, which represented an attempt to make archery more spectator friendly.

The Grand FITA format succeeded in doing one thing. It made archery harder to handicap and eventual winners less easy to predict, which added to the event's overall intrigue.

Grand FITA competition, as explained previously, requires female archers to shoot from distances of 30, 50, 60 and 70 meters.

Denise knew the rules. She knew about her competition, some only by name and deeds, and yet she realized perhaps better than anyone what she wanted to do and refused to let herself be intimidated no matter who she might face.

Denise Parker's parents had raised her with an attitude of 'prove yourself.' She knew that if she shot as well as she was capable of shooting then she belonged in the Olympics with all the other champions.

Even if she didn't shoot her absolute best, Denise never looked around her with awe and wondered if she really belonged in Seoul with the world's best archers.

"I belonged there," she said. "I knew that I could shoot with the best of them." ∎

Chapter 9

A Place in the Sun— and on the Podium

One Small Problem

No one seriously gave the U.S. women's archery team much of a chance to medal, despite the presence on the team of rising U.S. star, Denise Parker. In fact, prior to leaving for Seoul, the U.S. women's archery team had been ranked rather inauspiciously at ninth in the world.

Unbeknownst to many of those who'd followed her every move, Denise had been struggling with an equipment problem so thorny it was making her doubt herself. Easton Aluminum, the teen's sponsor, had recently developed the first aluminum/graphite composite arrows. The composites were lighter than the aluminum arrows Denise was accustomed to shooting. When shot from lighter draw weight bows composite arrows not only flew faster, they did so on a flatter (with less arc) trajectory. Easton was understandably eager for Denise to become proficient at shooting these arrows because if she did so and finished well up in the standings—or perhaps won a medal—her success would spur sales of the arrows around the globe. Strickland was also keenly awaiting Denise's mastery of the arrows. He, however, knew the arrows' increased speed would work to her competitive advantage, especially during windy conditions.

Here I am answering questions from the international press during a practice round at the Olympics in Seoul, South Korea.

Strickland and Denise worked together as they tweaked the teen's equipment one way and then the other, but inconsistent shot placement remained a problem. Denise's fiberglass recurve bow was now equipped with non-magnified sights and several chromed stabilizers. She carried a quiver and wore a chest protector, arm guard and finger tab for shooting. Equipment envy was a thing of the past as Denise would get whatever she needed to perform at the highest level.

Everything, that is, but the last crucial ingredient: the confidence that she could win with the arrows she was supposed to use. That confidence had gone missing when she and Strickland failed to work the bugs out of her equipment.

"I am going to do my best for my country, my parents and my friends back home," she'd told a reporter before she left South Jordan. Now that she was in Seoul, the questions tormenting her were, 'Will my best be good enough? Or will I let down everyone who's been counting on me?'

Trying her best was a given. For the first time, however, the ability to perform at the highest level she was capable of had become a concern. The 14-year-old grappled with the ramifications of her predicament on the eve of the most important competition of her life.

"Denise is one of the most technically perfect archers around, male or female," Strickland had often told reporters.

"When I tell her she can win she really doesn't see why she shouldn't win," Strickland continued. "I tell her to do something so she can shoot better and she does it."

Individual Rounds

On the first day of the individuals, held at Seoul's Hwarang Field, Denise's control seemed to have improved. She didn't shoot exceptionally well, but neither did she shoot that badly. By the conclusion of the two day open round, on September 28, in fact, Denise had shot 1,263 out of a perfect score of 1,440. Of the 62 archers who'd started the event, Denise finished in eleventh place, good enough to be one of the 24 qualifiers who would proceed to compete in the eighth round.

"I think she became a little nervous, standing next to the Russians, the Finns, and the Swedes," Earl Parker said, during one post-competition telephone interview. "I think (the experience) has been a little intimidating."

Intimidation gave way to frustration the next day when an erratic, swirling wind finished off any chance the teenager had of advancing again. The youngster, who on so many previous occasions had rewarded observers with her almost super-human accuracy, was revealed after all as mere mortal. Her score caused her to fall into twenty-first place, out of 24 archers. Eighteen archers would advance, but Denise wouldn't be one of them.

The Utahan's shooting hadn't been all that bad—her score was 298, out of 360, only 3 points under the 301 cutoff point that would have kept alive her individual medal quest. A poor score at 50-meters, where her nine arrows netted just 64 points, came back to haunt her, however.

The only American to advance to the quarterfinals was Melanie Skillman, 34, considered by many the team's weakest member. Skillman, however, scored 307 in the eighth round to

My coach, Tim Strickland, talking with me during a break in the Olympic competition.

A Teenage Archer's Quest for Olympic Glory

place 14th, which meant she moved on. Skillman continued shooting better than expected and eventually finished in the top 10, a superb accomplishment.

Practicing for the Team Competition

Denise had no time to ponder her failure, not with the U.S. women's team placing third in the qualification round, behind the Koreans and Russians, qualifying for the 12-team finals.

The strong team finish renewed the U.S. women's medal hopes. Denise, who shot her best when she had something to prove, this time could perhaps prove it to the most important person of all, herself.

Elimination in the individual competition only increased Denise's hunger for a better showing in the team competition.

"Debbie Ochs and I both became extremely motivated and focused," Denise said. "We both wanted to vindicate ourselves. We lived on the practice range for those few days waiting for the team round. You could say we got very focused."

Both Denise and Debbie felt they had something to prove.

The Team Competition

During the team event competitors would be shooting the Grand FITA. The first round—each team member must shoot nine arrows at distances of 30, 50, 60, and 70 meters. Contrary to all expectations, one of the teams to make it into the finals was team U.S.A.

"That morning when we started shooting everyone was shooting very, very well," Denise said. "We were so elated just to even make it into the finals."

The finals began that afternoon with all scores being wiped clean. Korea, Russia, Indonesia and the U.S. would be the main

Melanie, Debbie and me competing in the team competition at the 1988 Seoul Olympics.

contenders. The Indonesians briefly grabbed the early lead but quickly yielded it back to the incredibly talented Koreans. Halfway through the competition, the U.S. advanced into second place for just a short while, but mainly stayed in the third position.

A poor 50 meter performance hurt the Soviet team. The Soviets fell into fourth place, well behind the Americans. On the second to last end (of nine arrows), however, the Russians made up an incredible 13 points, which gave the Americans a momentary scare.

As the final last end got underway, Korea seemed to have the gold medal wrapped up. Their score was 901, so high that no other team could possibly match it. Indonesia, with 879, remained ahead of the Americans' 873 by six points, and ahead of Soviets by eight.

The American women shot for the last time. They could tell that their target (overall score) was good. Only one shot had been

My coach Tim Strickland and me after winning the bronze medal at the 1988 Seoul Olympic Games.

Melanie, me and Debbie on the stand to receive our Olympic Bronze Medals.

poor—a six, scored by Melanie Skillman.

The Americans then looked over at the Russians' target and could tell it looked as good—or perhaps even better—than theirs.

When the scores were tallied up the Russians had lost to the Americans by a single point, 951 to 952. Indonesia's score was exactly the same as the Americans'—952. A shoot off would be held between the U.S.A. and Indonesia to determine which team would win the silver medal and which the bronze.

During the day's competition the Americans had shot 216

Melanie, Debbie and me after receiving our medals.

arrows without missing the bale, or target. No one had even come close to doing so. But now, with silver on the line, Melanie Skillman shot and missed the entire target!

Skillman, who'd progressed further in the individual competition than any U.S. woman, suffered a meltdown with the silver medal on the line. Had her arrow hit almost anywhere on the target her team would have won silver medals.

Denise Parker

When the shoot off was over, Indonesia had 72 and the U.S. had 67.

The Americans were dejected, but only for a moment. They looked over at the Russians, who'd scored just one point less than they had, and knew they (the Americans) could have finished in

My mom, Valerie, and me celebrating after our bronze medal performance.

fourth place, and out of the medals, instead of in third.

"At first, we (the U.S. women) had this sense of having been so close to winning silver," Denise said. "That lasted a few seconds, and then we were thrilled we'd won any medal; even bronze felt great."

Ochs giggled and Denise smiled for a few minutes until the two archers noticed Melanie Skillman still appeared to be devastated by the recent miss of the entire target. Skillman briefly broke down and wept, but pulled herself out of it when she noticed how elated and supportive her teammates, coaches and the other Americans were.

Denise doesn't remember a lot about that magic moment in her life. "If I won an Olympic medal today—any Olympic medal— the experience would be burned into my memory," Denise said. "But I was 14. I knew I had my whole life ahead of me. I just knew—and so did my coaches—that there would be other Olympics and additional medals."

The media, however, weren't about to let Melanie forget the missed target, either, as they converged on the bronze medalists and bombarded them with questions about what might have been.

"If Melanie hadn't shot as well as she did earlier, we wouldn't have even been in contention for a silver medal," Denise reminded the press. "She did so much to get us there, and that's what counted most."

The Medals Ceremony

The announcer, confused by the American names, called them out backwards—"Parker Denise," the loudspeaker blared. No one cared, least of all the 14-year-old. Denise and her teammates were given bouquets by a Korean girl clad in a ceremonial silk kimono.

Denise Parker

And then it was time for Denise and her two teammates to step up onto the podium to receive their bronze medals as the flags of the three medaling countries almost simultaneously unfurled above them.

The band struck up the South Korean national anthem, and one can readily imagine at least one U.S. team member already thinking about how excited it would be, in four years, hence, when perhaps *The Star Spangled Banner* would be played at the conclusion of the 1992 archery competition at the Barcelona Olympics.

One could hardly fault the teenager for dreaming, not when she had a bronze medal, freshly earned, hanging around her neck. ■

Chapter 10
Struggling Under Expectations

The Once and Future Olympian

If Denise thought the media hype generated before the Olympics had been excessive, imagine her surprise when she stepped off of the jetliner to an even greater flood of attention. Demand for the '88 Games' youngest Olympian and youngest medalist couldn't have been higher, and it came from every quarter. The nation wanted to honor their Olympic medalists, and so did the state of Utah. Receptions were held, and then came the calls, scads of requests

My "welcome home" party my neighbors put on for me when I returned from the Olympics.

from TV and radio talk shows, conventions, business conglomerates and organizations, charities, everyone wanted a slice of Denise, whether to demonstrate her skill with a bow, give a motivational speech or make a personal appearance. An agent was finally hired to sort through the offers even though letters and declarations continued to flood the Parker home, including another from the President of the United States, George Herbert Walker Bush. Only after about six months did the excitement start to die down. By then, Denise was more than ready to relinquish the spotlight.

Not that she wasn't grateful to archery and for what the sport had done for her. She'd visited countries and encountered people from all over the globe, including the Far East, Asia, Europe and South America. She'd met Olympic gold medal diver Greg Louganis, one of her teen idols, and had been honored at a reception in honor of Louganis, ice-skater Holly Cook, and other Utah Olympians, including herself. Thanks to parents who had done what they could to keep fame from turning their daughter's fair head, as well as her own natural aversion to attention, the teenager enjoyed a fairly average high school experience during the next four years.

Not completely average, of course, because no matter how one might parse the situation, Denise was an Olympian and would remain one until her dying day. She was a member of one of the world's most elite clubs. Denise, however, was not only just an Olympian, but one of the chosen few who'd actually won a medal.

Dares and bets continued to motivate her, however; proving that it was just part of the teen's inherent psychological make-up. When Denise turned 16 and was old enough to get her driver's license, her father challenged her to shoot another 1,300. If she did, Earl Parker said he'd get Denise a car.

Once the bet had been made and its terms agreed upon, Denise, in April, 1989, journeyed to Arizona where she set two additional national records. She shot 1,314 in a Grand FITA, breaking her previous record of 1,301. She also set a single shoot 60-meter record with a score of 331, which bettered by one point her previous record of 330.

Earl paid up, in a manner of speaking. Rather than purchase his daughter a car, however, he bequeathed upon the girl his wife's 10-year-old Renault Alliance. Denise didn't care. She owned a car, and that was good enough for her.

Earl had planned to get Denise something better than the Renault, but discovered the sporty model he'd had in mind was beyond his financial reach. Without Denise knowing, Earl approached Easton Aluminum to negotiate a new sponsorship contract, which he succeeded in doing. One of the contract's terms: a new red sports car, a Toyota Celica, for Denise.

"That was pretty cool," Denise said. "I had this neat car while I was still in high school, and I owed it all to archery."

Blending In

Only one South Jordan teenager had won an Olympic bronze medal and, with it, worldwide acclaim and fame. That teenager had been

One of the many parades I was part of upon my return home.

feted, upon her return from Seoul, on Denise Parker Day by over a thousand friends and classmates from Bingham Middle School which had been decorated in her honor. That evening a dance, with strobe lights and D.J., was held in her honor.

After all the hoopla, how did Denise cope when the time came to return to classes and sports teams with her friends? Would friends and new acquaintances ever again consider her just one of the crowd?

"Playing school sports (at Bingham Middle and High Schools, both in South Jordan) helped ease my way back into everyday life," explained Denise.

As she'd done so many times before, Denise threw herself into competitive sports like basketball, softball and soccer. She wanted to win in school sports as much as she'd ever wanted to win tournaments, and as fiercely as did her teammates. The kids who comprised her teams soon seemed to forget Denise had an Olympic medal. She was simply a teammate who gave her all to whatever sport she was playing, and that was what mattered most.

Competing in high school sports meant as much to me at the time as training for the Olympics.

A Teenage Archer's Quest for Olympic Glory

Me competing in the World Championships in Lausanne, Switzerland where I finished third.

Denise could be herself with these friends. They grew to depend upon her—and she upon them—to celebrate wins and suffer defeats. Denise continued to rely upon her network of teammates throughout her high school years. They served as her life support system and social safety net, in many ways, and had come to her aid when she needed them most, which was during the time she needed to restore the normalcy to her life that too often, lately, had been lacking.

Boys, Boys, Boys

Denise was probably the only girl in her high school to receive regular fan mail from boys. Letters, with photos included, arrived fairly regularly to ask their recipient out on dates. Denise found such incidents slightly disconcerting.

Denise Parker

"The cool guy from your own high school won't date you, but the one across the state, the one you've never met and don't know, he'd give anything to take you out," Denise complained.

Not that Denise had trouble finding boys to date. Joe Borich, a star athlete at her high school, asked her out and the two became high school sweethearts. Borich was something of a big man on campus. He played quarterback for the varsity football team and was a member of the varsity baseball and basketball teams.

"I did all right" (in the boy department), Denise laughed.

Charging Toward the Summit

Records, meanwhile, continued to topple as Denise charged onward during her high school years toward what was hoped would be a gold medal effort in the 1992 Olympic Games in Barcelona.

A year after winning the bronze medal, during the 1989 U. S. National Indoor Archery Championships, in Salt Lake City, the 15-year-old set seven national records. One also was certified as the event's new world record.

Denise's scores in that meet were better than those of 1988 Olympic gold medalist Jay Barrs, of Arizona, two-time Olympian Rick McKinney, of Arizona, and two-time Olympian Ed Eliason, also of Utah. During the women's 18 meter event, Denise shot 587. Of the 60 arrows she shot, 47 landed in the bull's eye, a circle smaller than a silver dollar, while the other 13 landed in the slightly larger nine-ring.

Denise also competed in that year's World Championships competition in Switzerland (1989). She shot a 338 in one round, her best score ever for such a round, or pass. Among the 36 arrows she shot, 19 were bull's eyes. She placed third, her highest individual finish ever in international competition.

The teenager, however, considered her third place showing somewhat

A Teenage Archer's Quest for Olympic Glory

The award ceremony where I received my bronze medal from the World Championships.

ruefully. "I may not have expected to finish third (in the Olympics), like I did in this World Championship competition," she explained. "But I didn't expect to finish 21st, either (where she finished in the individual competition). That was a big disappointment."

A disappointment that the teenager would now try to forget. She got off to a good start by finishing third at the Worlds. Two years later, when she was 17, she traveled to Norway where she won the Junior World Championships. She decided to compete because even though she had won senior titles, this would be the last year, because of her age, she'd be able to enter the tournament.

"I was shooting my best between the ages of 15 and 18," Denise said.

The End of a Partnership

Earl Parker had long been Denise's rock, the person to whom she looked for encouragement when she was feeling down, and for guidance when she occasionally failed to shoot her best. He'd always been in her corner, through good times and times not so good, and both

Denise Parker

The award ceremony where I was crowned Junior World Champion in Norway.

father and daughter believed that in her corner Earl would remain.

Winning the Olympic bronze medal at age 14 hadn't, however, changed Denise's life alone. It had changed Earl Parker's life as well.

Put yourself in his shoes, for a moment. Think of the glory reflected back at him, from his daughter's many accomplishments, in which the man could rightly bask. It was he, after all, who had been at Denise's side from the very beginning, he who'd bought her the first bow, and he who'd found the instructor who gave his daughter those first lessons on the path to archery greatness.

Denise may have had many archery coaches during her brief career, but she had just one who shared the same last name. Earl knew her better than anyone, or so people—including Earl—seemed to think. Earl also felt he knew what was best for Denise, no matter what the circumstances.

One can forgive him for these lines of thinking. For if Denise was the athlete who performed beyond anyone's expectations, wouldn't it be safe to state that Earl had been the overseer who'd made certain that Denise trained with the right coaches, got the proper rest and psychological training, and otherwise did his best to fill in as coach, motivator, trainer and even physical therapist when no one else was available to do so?

Whether rightly or wrongly, Earl along with much of the archery world felt he deserved some credit for making Denise into the competitor she'd become. His daughter had won Olympic bronze. She'd won the Junior World Championships, at age 17, and he knew she had an excellent chance again of running away with that year's U.S. Nationals. He'd remained by her side during all that time, and he could be excused for believing that once the right combination of carrot—reward—and stick—work or practice—was found, Denise would win Olympic gold in Barcelona.

Earl and Denise arrived in Ohio two days before the 1991 U.S. Archery National Championships competition were scheduled to begin. The Parkers usually arrived early so Denise could walk the field, do some shooting and generally get a feel for conditions on the actual field where the competition would take place.

Another reason the Parkers had arrived early was to give Earl the opportunity to gauge the quality of Denise's shooting. Denise had been experiencing something of a rough patch with her shooting, and Earl wasn't pleased because he knew she should be shooting much better.

Denise wasn't worried. She'd weathered temporary declines in accuracy or consistency before, and she knew she'd overcome this one as well.

Denise began to shoot. Earl waited nearby and offered occasional comments and suggestions. The teenager continued to shoot from about 9 a.m. until the pair broke for lunch at noon.

After lunch, Earl told Denise that she should continue to practice.

"I never liked to shoot much prior to a competition because I didn't want to tire myself out," explained Denise.

Denise, however, agreed and went back out onto the range where she continued to shoot until the field was shut down for the evening. She then put down her bow, gathered up her gear and started packing it away.

"What are you doing?" Earl asked.

"Putting my bow away," Denise replied.

"No, you're not," Earl countered. "You're going to the practice field to shoot some more.

"No, I'm not," said Denise. "I'm worn out. I've shot all day and I'm not going to shoot any more."

Earl Parker was stunned. His daughter, the youngster who he'd loved as his own and on whom he'd lavished so much time and energy, had refused his request to practice some more. This, he could neither understand nor tolerate. He turned and started walking toward their hotel.

Denise continued loading her equipment into the car. When she was finished she climbed in behind the wheel and drove the car to where she could see her father walking ahead of her.

"Dad, get in the car," she said.

Earl said nothing. Nor would he look at Denise. He simply continued walking toward the hotel while he considered his words carefully.

"I don't think you fully appreciate what I've tried to do for you," Earl finally said.

Denise knew the sacrifices her parents had made for her. Her father, especially, had willingly done more than ninety-nine percent of the world's fathers would have had they found themselves in a similar position.

Denise, in her defense, had quietly suffered the loss of the father she'd idolized, and his replacement by Earl Parker, no-nonsense coach. The man who'd stood beside her, offering encouragement and praise, in good times and bad had gradually morphed since the Pan

Am Games into a rather stern taskmaster whom with each passing day it was becoming more difficult to please.

Denise followed as her father walked to their room. She waited silently while he packed his bags. When he was finished, he told his daughter that she should remain in Ohio for the competition. He, meanwhile, would continue onward to West Virginia, where his mother still lived and where he would stay until the competition was over. And then he left. Denise had been alone before, but never as alone as she was at that moment.

Lesser competitors under similar duress might have flinched and lost. Not Denise. She put on her business-as-usual game face, stepped to the firing line and won the U. S. Nationals.

Would she be so stoic when she once again had to face her father?

Nothing more passed between them until after they'd returned to South Jordan. Denise, who'd been thinking about what she would tell her father, decided to unburden her heart and hoped Earl would understand her reasons for doing so.

"Dad, I don't want you to coach me anymore," she said. "I need a father, not a coach. Having you coach me just isn't worth the strain on our relationship."

Earl's world shattered as he listened to her words. He'd completely dedicated himself to her career and now felt as though he'd been set adrift. He was still her father, but it was painfully clear that Denise no longer would permit him to be her coach. He'd been displaced as the nucleus of her world and relegated instead to circle along its periphery in rather aimless fashion. At the moment, being told his future function would be solely as Denise's father felt a lot like a demotion.

Denise, on the other hand, thought that having Earl around—as her father—to offer unconditional love and support, whether she won in glorious fashion or suffered ignominious defeat, was worth more than countless world-class coaches. Coaches, she knew, might come and go, but she hoped her father would be by her side forever.

"My father became terribly upset," said Denise, as she recalled one of the worst times of her life. "But I'd made up my mind. I was in high school. I now had my own life and my own car and at that age, you feel like that's all you need. When I was younger, I would have been forced to reconsider what I'd said, but not now. I'd grown up and I knew what I wanted."

Deja Vú All Over Again

Denise could be excused if, in later years, she looked back on this portion of her life to think she was living the Bill Murray lead in the movie *Groundhog Day*. Each day, Murray, playing the part of a rather obnoxious jerk (which Denise wasn't), would wake up to discover it was Groundhog Day. He was such a jerk, *karma* or God or fate must have decided he had to relive the day, over and over again, until he finally got it right. So, too, Denise must have noticed similarities between the months that had led her up to the 1988 Olympics and those she was now living and which would lead, perhaps, to a slot on the 1992 Olympic team. The same tournaments were once again appearing on her schedule, including the Pan American Games and the Olympic Festival.

One thing had changed, however: Denise was no longer the youngest archer in competition at those tournaments. "In a way I was glad to get rid of (that distinction)," she said. "I was getting tired of being the youngest everything."

With age and increased maturity, however, came more pressure to win. Denise now stood 5 feet 6 inches tall and weighed 120 pounds, which was six inches taller and about 30 pounds heavier than she'd been four years previously. Competing at the highest level meant not only maintaining her accuracy but finding ways to improve her shooting, which was a constant challenge.

The 1991 Pan Am Games were held in Havana, Cuba. The archery competition, however, took place in Santiago, far from Fidel Castro's courtside seat. Castro's presence, some competitors would later claim, had been an unwelcome distraction during the Games. Denise, fortunately, did not have to contend with Castro's presence at the archery venue and, indeed, must have found the languid island air and sea breezes to her liking as she thoroughly dominated the competition to win five Pan Am gold medals and a silver. Piracy could easily have been claimed in the islands where pirates enjoyed their brief heyday, because Denise basically plundered the other contestants to take gold in the women's individual competition and the team competition, and also won individual gold medals at 30 meters, 60 meters and 70 meters (distance medals were something new to the Pan Am Games). Her lone silver had nearly been golden as well. She was tied for first at the end of the 50 meter round, but came up short in the tiebreaker.

She was at the peak of her game and the apex of her powers. During one interview, she revealed the secret of getting into 'The Zone,' "You just try to be brain dead when you shoot. You keep all your thoughts on the target." Denise, by this time, was well-versed in the technique. She knew the instant a potential shot 'felt' right. Her intense training combined with superior mental control derived from years of psychological exercises helped her recognize the moment to let instincts and training take over. Denise Parker, her competitors were discovering with dismay, was in The Zone more often these days then than out of it.

The End of Her High School Years

Denise's superior performance in the 1992 Olympic Trials was of utmost importance to her, and had been considered throughout her high school years whenever it was time to select an upcoming semester's course load. Judicious selection of her courses meant that she had enough credits to graduate early. She could take off the final semester of her senior year to concentrate wholly on the Trials and still graduate with honors.

She also could look back with pride at a high school sojourn during which she'd encouraged varsity coaches to treat her the same as her teammates. She wanted no exceptions made, simply because she was a famous archer. As a starter on the Utah state championship girls' basketball team, she had her share of travails as she tried to mesh archery with academics and other high school activities.

Rand Rasmussen, Denise's Bingham High basketball coach, had issued an edict that stated any player who missed practice would not be permitted to play in the following game. Denise, who was integral to her team's success as the starting point guard, knew she had to compete in Las Vegas the week before the team would be playing for the state championship.

"I practiced basketball on Thursday afternoon, flew to Las Vegas Thursday evening and competed Friday morning," Denise recalled. "I then flew back to practice with my team Friday afternoon and Saturday morning. I then caught a flight back to Las Vegas so I could shoot Saturday afternoon. I competed in the finals on Sunday morning and returned home immediately afterward.

"My Dad became angry about all this flying back and forth," Denise continued. "But we won the state championship, and I won the competition.

"I respected Coach Rasmussen for the way he handled the situation. He'd made it clear: if you were going to be a part of the team you would be a part of the team. The team came first. You had to respect the team and your teammates whether or not you were an Olympic archer. That was just the way it was and the way it should have been.

My high school basketball team, the Bingham Miners, took the state championship in 1990.

If I wanted to play, I had to play by the rules. I didn't want to be favored, for any reason at all."

The 1992 Olympic Trials

Denise now was shooting a 64-inch composite recurve bow, just two inches shorter than she was tall, which weighed six pounds. The bow, like the arrows that had been somewhat troublesome in Seoul, was made of material that was a composite of wood, fiberglass and carbon compounds. Its draw weight of 34 pounds was high enough to propel one of Denise's arrows toward a target at speeds up to 150 miles per hour. Even in 1992, her arrows, had she bought them, would have cost $13 apiece. Her bow, if purchased on the open market, would have retailed for about $1,000, quite a hefty sum even now.

Archers competing at Barcelona in 1992 would also have to adjust to a new competitive format called the FITA Olympic round. The preliminary qualification round was conducted over two days and required archers to shoot 144 arrows from the various specified distances. The 32 top-scoring archers, however, would then be seeded by their scores and placed in a tournament draw. Depending on draw results, each archer would then compete one-on-one with another, each shooting 18 arrows per match at 70 meters, until the quarter finals where they would shoot 12-arrow matches until an overall winner emerged. Olympic organizers had again changed the format in hopes of increasing worldwide TV viewership by making archery both more accessible and more exciting.

Denise was happy to hear that match play in the final rounds would determine the winner. The change would prevent her strongest international rivals, the Koreans, from building up insurmountable leads in the early going.

The 17-year-old entered that year's Olympic Trials with few cares in the world. She'd been shooting phenomenally, and her confidence had never been higher. The archery gods—and goddesses—must have been smiling down from Mount Olympus, since even the format of the upcoming Games had been modified in a way that seemed to play to Denise's competitive advantage.

Everyone hoped that The Olympic Festival, held in Encino, California, would provide a preview of what would transpire in Barcelona the following August. Denise outshot everyone to win the gold with a score of 339. Terry Quinn, of Houston, garnered 319 points and Kitty Frazier, West Virginia, scored 317. On the men's side Ed Eliason scored 333 to take the gold, while Gerald Pylpchuk, of New Jersey, scored 328 and Jay Barrs, of Arizona, was third with 326.

No U. S. competitor, it seemed, could challenge Denise's dominance. She crushed everyone at The Olympic Trials to make the team. Her teammates would be Jennifer O'Donnell and Sherry Block. Jennifer was the same age as Denise and already a friend since the two had competed in many of the same competitions. Having a friend her own

A Teenage Archer's Quest for Olympic Glory

age again seemed to bode well for her future Olympic hopes. Sherry, however, had come out of nowhere to make the team. Prior to the Trials, Janet Dykman had been expected to round out the women's team, since Denise and Janet had for several years consistently finished most tournaments in first and second places respectively.

Denise certainly harbored no ill will toward Sherry Block, and yet knowing Janet and her capabilities as well as she did made the next couple of months difficult, particularly when everyone—Denise included—knew that the team's best chance for a medal was in the team event.

"It's difficult when you know someone as well as I knew Janet and then she doesn't make the team," explained Denise. "I didn't know Sherry well, but I knew she'd had a good score at the Trials." Denise and Jennifer both hoped that good score would translate into a fine performance in Barcelona.

Several international competitions loomed between the Trials and the Olympics. As might have been expected, Denise and Jennifer became inseparable. Competing together for so many years had made the teenagers pals, and their good chemistry now got even better.

Sherry, through no fault of her own, other than shooting well enough at the Trials to make the team, which is hardly a 'fault,' was never able to penetrate Denise and Jennifer's inner circle. Sherry, who was in her 30s, was quite a bit older than the teens. Adding to the girls' impression of her as something of an 'outsider' was knowing that in past competitions Sherry had lacked consistency, and consistency, the friends knew, is what wins tournaments and medals.

The 1992 Olympic Games: Barcelona, Spain

Denise went into the 1992 Olympics ranked ninth in the world. No longer was she the youngest archer, nor was she an unknown—and largely untested—commodity as she'd been in Seoul four years previously. The world had seen her skyrocket to the top of her game and, as Tim Strickland had stated, there was no telling how high she someday might climb.

A ranking of ninth, while impressive, still means eight of the world's female archers are considered better than you are. Whether that assessment was correct or incorrect didn't matter much to Denise. Winning an individual Olympic medal would have surprised most of the tight-knit archery world, but that's exactly what she aimed to do. She would simply shoot her best, and hope that her best would be good enough for a medal.

Denise continued to see the format change as an advantage.

"I'm not sure I could stay with Kim (Soo-Nyung, the defending Olympic champion from Korea) for 144 arrows," explained Denise, at the time. "I know, however, that I can shoot 12 arrows as well as anyone. So that improves my chances against her. But then again, someone can do to me what I want to do to her."

The process of being outfitted for and traveling to the 1992 Games was very similar to what Denise had experienced in 1988. "The clothes, once again, were fantastic," she recalled.

Barcelona's Olympic Village was memorable for a couple of reasons. First, there was a bowling alley for the athletes, and second, the Village had been built on a beach and part of that beach was open only to Olympians. "Those things were pretty cool," she said.

It was only her second time at the Olympics but already Denise felt like she was an old hand at the Games. Whether that feeling also would be an advantage was yet to be seen. ■

Chapter 11
The Meltdown

Let the Games Begin

When an archer was selected to light the Olympic flame during Barcelona's opening ceremonies, Denise considered it a harbinger of good luck to come, both for her individual efforts as well as the team's.

Why wouldn't she, considering how well everything had gone leading up to this moment. She had a roommate she liked and who was the same age, Olympic Village seemed somehow better

Me and other members of the 1992 U.S. Archery Olympic Team.
Back: Coach Dick Tone, Butch Johnson, Jay Barrs and manager Judy Rabsko
Front: me, Jennifer O'Donnell and Sherry Block. Teammate Rick McKinney not shown.

than before, or perhaps it just seemed more comfortable and familiar. Olympic Village even had a McDonald's where she could nosh or just hang out with friends.

Had she been asked if there was any way to improve the experience, Denise may have offered just one suggestion: start the archery competition much earlier. As scheduled, the archers would have to cool their heels while nearly every other event was conducted and the winners decided upon. Only two competitions would start later than archery—water polo and canoeing.

Me competing at the 1992 Olympics in Barcelona, Spain.

Here I am shooting in the 1992 Olympic quarter-final match against Valeeva.

The nuts and bolts of why and how Barcelona was selected mattered less to the U. S. archery team than when their competition would get underway. Waiting for the competition to begin was like watching paint dry; it seemed like it would never happen. Friday, August 7, 1992, arrived at last and with it the first day of what was to be two days of qualifying rounds. The 32 women who survived elimination and remained in contention at the end of Saturday's qualifying would, under the new Olympic FITA format, move on to the finals on Sunday.

If Denise, however, had believed her main competition would come at the hands of Korean Soo-Nyung Kim, the gold medalist in Seoul, she soon discovered otherwise. After the first day of qualifying not one Korean stood between Denise and an individual medal, but three. Youn-Jeong Cho started red hot. Cho charged out front to set an Olympic record of 345 from 60 meters, and a world record of 338 from 70 meters. Finishing in second and third places respectively, were two more Koreans, Soo-Nyung Kim and Eun-Kyung Lee.

Denise, meanwhile, finished the day quite respectably in fifth place with a score of 659. Natalia Valeeva, of the Unified (Russian) Team, was in fourth, positioned between the trio of Koreans and Denise.

Denise's 70 meter score of 328 had been the fourth best of the morning. Had she not shot one poor end of 49 (out of a possible 60) she would have been in second place behind Youn-Jeong Cho.

Jennifer O'Donnell, meanwhile, had finished twenty-fourth overall at 628. Sherry Block was in serious danger of being cut with a score of 621, which relegated her to thirty-second place. Only 32 archers would proceed to Sunday's 70-meter one-on-one shoot-off.

Denise now went head-to-head with the world's best and never flinched. Her arrows found the bull's eyes, round after round, until she'd advanced to the quarterfinals or top eight. There she was matched up with Natalia Valeeva, of the Unified Team.

As luck would have it, Denise and Natalia would be the first pairing to shoot in the quarterfinals using the brand new Olympic alternating format (first one archer shoots, and then the other. The second archer then shoots first, followed by the first archer, and so forth).

"Natalia and I were going head-to-head," said Denise. "I was down to my final three arrows and ahead in points. If I could get past (Natalia) I would be in the top four and have an excellent chance of winning an individual medal. Winning a gold medal would have been great, but even as excited as I was I knew the gold was unlikely since Korea was so dominant.

"I shot two arrows and still was 3 points ahead," Denise continued. "I knew I only had to hit the 8-ring to tie, the 9-ring or better to win."

Denise was no stranger to 'do-or-die' situations. She'd been in stomach-knotting matches before, many with a tournament or a championship, or even a gold medal on the line. This, however, was different and she knew it. This match might very well lead to Olympic gold.

"I felt confident," she said. "I wasn't nervous. I wasn't even feeling that much pressure. I truly believed I'd win the match. I pulled back the string, aimed and knew that this was the shot. It felt good. I released the string and, in that instant, I knew I'd won!"

But Denise hadn't won. She hadn't even tied. Her arrow rather inexplicably had veered into the 6-ring. She'd lost. There would be no next round, and no individual Olympic medal, either.

"I was devastated," said Denise. "I couldn't believe it. I'd been in competitions where I was so nervous I couldn't feel my legs. I'd sometimes become so stressed that I'd briefly lose all muscle strength. This, however, hadn't been one of those times."

The media was relentless after the match. They clustered around the American, firing question after question, along with one or two questions predominating. "Did you choke?" went one favorite. "Was the pressure too much to bear?"

"I said it then and I still believe it today: I felt confident, not nervous," stated Denise. "I didn't choke. I think, perhaps, at the last second I anticipated the win. At that instant, I may have lost my focus.

"I finished fifth," she continued. I ordinarily would have been extremely happy with that, but not this time. I knew—and so did everyone else—that I'd been so very close, and yet hadn't come through when it counted most."

Aftermath

Denise has had years to replay, over and over in her mind, the crushing moment. In some ways, she admitted, she will never be free of it.

"Thinking back, I believe I was looking for my arrow (where it would hit) before I ever shot," she explained. "I rushed it. It's my own fault."

One reporter asked if she'd ever before suffered similar moments.

"Not like this," she replied. "These are the *Olympics.*"

Four more years. The phrase became Denise's mantra as she now began looking ahead to 1996, once more so far in the future.

"I blew it. Anything in the gold ring would have done it, but I was so excited I couldn't wait to see where it went."

Denise bravely shouldered the blame, despite an extenuating circumstance that provides a plausible reason for her failure that day. That was the order in which each pair of arrows was to have been shot by Denise and Natalia.

At the beginning of the shoot-off a coin flip determined who would shoot first. Denise won the toss, and elected to shoot first.

This method was traditionally used in head-to-head matches prior to 1992. As originally conceived and executed, the archer who shot first would continue shooting first throughout each arrow pairing and including the final pair of arrows.

That rule had been modified, earlier that year. It now stated that the coin toss winner could choose the shooting order for only the first arrow. Once the first pair of arrows was shot, the coin toss winner must then alternate shooting order, for each subsequent pair of arrows, with the other archer. Denise, in other words, would have shot the first arrow, followed by Natalia. The shooting order would then alternate with the next pair of arrows: Natalia would shoot first, followed by Denise.

Denise had always known about the change and everyone had always chose the option that would put their competitor shooting the last arrow. 'Last arrow pressure' is a tried-and-true tactic archers use to rattle their opponents during the head-to-head competitions. However, at the moment of the coin toss, she had lapsed back and inadvertently chosen the wrong selection. Denise elected to shoot first because she thought that by doing so she'd force Valeeva to shoot last. In this instance, however, Denise inadvertently placed last arrow pressure upon herself, and was somewhat taken aback when she discovered what she had done. "Part of being a competitor is knowing the rules. I should have known the rule and there was no excuse for the mistake." She states of the incident. She'd graciously accepted all of her many triumphs, and she knew it was now imperative to accept this defeat equally as graciously and move on.

Moving on, however, would prove surprisingly difficult for the young woman who had accomplished so much in just eight years.

The Bitter Truth

Up until that awful moment when the anticipated failed to materialize, Denise's reign as queen of U. S. archery had been characterized by her fearlessness, no matter what the situation.

"Up until that day in Barcelona I shot without fear," she acknowledged. "I never thought about the consequences of failure. I just shot and was confident of my abilities."

Afterwards, however, doubts began to plague her. "I wondered if I was as good as I'd once thought," Denise admitted. "I worried about my ability to deal with unrelenting pressure. I even wondered if perhaps I'd choked that day. The experience of prematurely believing that I'd won, when I'd actually lost, had been so awful, and the day so terrible overall, I knew I'd forever worry that it would happen again."

She worried despite almost carrying the women's team to another Olympic team medal. The U. S. women made it into the quarterfinals only to be ousted by France, 232 to 225.

Denise returned home with nothing to show for her efforts. She felt like she'd lost despite finishing fifth in the qualifying FITA round, making it to the quarterfinals of the individuals and scoring 10s with the last three arrows she'd shot during the team competition. But she felt like an abject failure and, as sages are fond of saying, 'Perception is everything.'

In other words, perceive yourself as a failure and you soon might become one.

Denise later admitted as much. "I really don't think I ever fully recovered from what happened that day (against Valeeva)," she said.

Denise felt as though her life in archery had shattered that day in Barcelona. And yet, despite the loss, she was ranked fifth in the world.

"I didn't see myself as being somehow above the problem of dealing with pressure," explained Denise. "I'd dealt with pressure before and won. It doesn't matter if the pressure comes at the club (local) level, the state level, the nationals or on the world stage. Someone unable to handle pressure will never make it to the Olympics. Each of my competitors in Barcelona had dealt with pressure—and handled it, too—or they wouldn't have been there with me."

Denise had never before doubted herself, and the media hadn't either. She'd been their darling, so to read or hear what reporters or news anchors were writing or saying about the quarterfinal debacle, when most had never shot a bow in their lives, was off-putting to say the least. So was hearing the whispers that suddenly ceased when you came near.

Worst of all, perhaps, was the near-constant worry it would happen again. Maybe not tomorrow or perhaps not even the next day, but what about at some important competition in the as yet unforeseeable future? She would be up there, the eyes of the world upon her, with what? An Olympic medal hanging in the balance? Perhaps. Denise only knew that merely imagining such a future scenario—and what might happen—was almost too terrible to contemplate.

On some level, Denise knew that to harbor such dreads or worries was futile in the extreme.

"That's what living is," remarked Denise. Continuing onward in the face of adversity and, yes, even doubt. "It can be difficult sometimes, however, to put that attitude into action," she said.

"My failure to accomplish what I knew I was capable of really got to me," she continued. "It preyed on my mind and caused me to struggle afterwards. I continued to shoot well, but I never fully recovered mentally. Before that day mental toughness had been one of my finest competitive attributes. But afterwards, no matter what I did or how I tried to approach it I found I'd lost that mental toughness." Never again, regrettably, would Denise consider herself to be as mentally tough as she once was.

College

Denise graduated with honors from Bingham High School. Denise's high school grades and college entrance scores had been high enough to attract the offer of a partial academic scholarship to Southern Utah University, located in Cedar City. Denise accepted the scholarship and when she traveled to the university she encountered Becky Schofield, a girl she'd known while playing high school basketball.

"Becky recommended that I try out as a walk-on for the basketball team," said Denise. "I did, and I made the team."

Denise kept herself busy at Southern Utah playing on the women's varsity basketball team and continued in archery. She remained at Southern Utah from 1992 to 1994, and then took off the next year to dedicate herself to training for the 1996 Olympics.

Dealing

Denise continued to struggle mentally, and even perhaps emotionally, as she attempted to come to grips with what ailed her before the qualifying for the 1996 Olympics. Despite her monumental case of self-doubt, Denise continued to excel as an archer. She won her third U. S. World Archery Championship Trials, and then followed that up by shooting the highest score of her life — 1,361 — at the 1993 World Championships in Turkey. That score would prove so high no American woman has yet surpassed it, or even equaled it. During the two days of qualifying at the Worlds, Denise went up against the Russians, the Koreans and others and beat them all. In head-to-head competition, however, she was eliminated in the second round and finished in twentieth place overall.

She'd banished her father from her archery life, and now contemplated doing the same with Tim Strickland.

"I couldn't help but wonder if Tim was the best coach for me," she explained. "Things definitely weren't working out for me, and, in retrospect, it was probably easier to blame my problems on others than on myself, where the blame belonged."

The rough spot she'd hit with her father, at the 1991 U. S. Nationals, had failed to become any smoother, and that also preyed on Denise's mind.

The people Denise knew, naturally, were anxious to help her return to championship form. Many gave her advice, much of which only added to her confusion. Some told her she'd never return to top form because she wouldn't dedicate herself solely to archery. These folks thought that playing basketball, soccer and softball, in addition to archery, was too much of a load as well as major distractions for someone who aspired to be the best in the world.

Advice flew at the young woman from every direction, and yet most observers agreed that 1996 would be her year *if* she trained hard and exclusively in archery. After all, or so the reasoning went, the 1996 Olympics would be held in Atlanta, in the United States, Denise's home turf. Nocking arrows at home, where the crowd would be solidly in her corner, where long days of travel, jet lag, unfamiliar surroundings and strange foods would no longer be factors would have to weigh in her favor.

Denise convinced herself that what she was hearing made perfect sense, "I told myself that 1996 would be my year."

Total Dedication

Denise set about her training regimen with a mindset like none she'd had before. She analyzed her previous years of training and decided that she'd never trained hard enough, never as much as other Olympians, and that was why she'd never done better than she had.

She'd taken a leave of absence from college, so she packed up clothing and gear and moved into a new Olympic training center in San Diego where she became a resident athlete. She had one thing—and one thing only on her mind: to train as hard as she could.

She began each day with a run of between three and six miles, then shoot 150 to 200 arrows during a morning archery session and break for lunch. Tim Strickland was still in the picture, but Denise

My roommate Courtney Kane and me at the U.S. Olympic Training Center in Chula Vista, California.

had also started receiving instructions from various coaches.

"I got advice and instruction from several different coaches during that time, which wasn't very smart," Denise admitted. "But I was determined to find the magic fix that would solve my problems and take me to the top."

Each afternoon Denise would shoot another 150-200 arrows. After all, she'd heard that her Korean rivals shot more than 300 arrows each day, and she was determined to beat them, if only in the number of arrows shot each day at practice. She trained three days each week with weights, consulted regularly with a sports psychologist, maintained a meticulous daily journal detailing each day's performance, including training regimen, coach of the day and notes about her mental attitude. In essence, she tried to do whatever was feasible to heap even more pressure upon herself.

"My actions, in effect, were saying, 'Okay, I'm doing all these things. I'd better see improvement.'"

Denise shot and she shot and she shot some more. But rather than improve, her once-legendary accuracy now declined. But instead of relaxing or taking it easier, she'd force herself to shoot even more arrows. The downward spiral continued.

"I began to hate archery," Denise commented. "Not only was I spinning out of control, I seemed to be spiraling downward as fast as I could go. I saw no way out, either."

Qualifying for the 1996 Olympics

Denise was now 22. She'd be a junior when she returned to college someday, but she had taken a year off to concentrate exclusively on the sport that was now both compulsion and obsession. The vision that had once allowed her to see and encompass life, in all its many glorious facets, unfolding around her and sweeping her up in its joy now narrowed until she could see her objective in only the narrowest sense. Just one thing appeared within her field of view, and that was Olympic gold.

That year's Trials would consist of three different competitions. Competitors would shoot in one event, to be held in Ohio. If they qualified there they would proceed to the next event in Long Beach, California. From Long Beach, the qualifiers would move on to what could be termed the Olympic Trials finals where the three top-scoring men and women would be awarded berths on the 1996 Olympic team.

Denise performed well enough in Ohio to move on to Long Beach. She was highly ranked, at the time, but on that day ranking counted for nothing. Everything would hinge on her performance in Long Beach.

"I felt I *had* to win," said Denise. "I tried harder and harder, but it made me tense and unable to relax. I was unable to just let my ability take over. I was forcing everything, nothing seemed natural."

Denise, who had always been able to get through difficult situations, found herself unable to find her focus. "I was in pure panic mode. I had completely lost all confidence and I was totally obsessed with being scared of shooting bad. I knew I wasn't going to make the team. It was the worst experience of my life."

She was right. She lost and was eliminated from contention. There would be no chance for redemption in Atlanta.

"I went home, threw my bow into a corner and said, 'I hate archery, I hate competition and I never want to shoot again.'"

Valerie Parker felt her daughter's pain, but knew nothing she said could make it stop hurting.

Earl Parker said nothing at all. He'd felt pain of his own in 1991. Denise, he knew, was so upset with herself and her performance that anything he might have said couldn't have made it hurt any worse than it already did nor could he make her feel better. ∎

Chapter 12
The Comeback

Away from the Spotlight

Denise kept her word. She abandoned archery as thoroughly and as completely as she'd embraced it eight years earlier. The psychological struggles she'd tried to battle through, added to the years of intense training and the titanic four year wait until she once again was able to try to prove herself by making another Olympic team, had taken a

I graduated from Westminster College in Salt Lake City, Utah in 1997.

drastic toll on her. When she quit, she willingly melted into the background where she inhabited an unobtrusive place that suited her just fine.

Money garnered as a result of contracts with archery sponsors or from winning competitions was used to help pay for her education at Southern Utah University. She enjoyed her years in Cedar City, but when the time came to return to college she decided to apply to the rather exclusive Westminster College in Salt Lake City. Westminster was pricey but it was an excellent school, one that Denise admits she would have been unable to attend had it not been for her earnings from archery.

Denise graduated from Westminster in 1997 with a degree in marketing. Her first job was working as an account representative for an advertising agency where she met with clients and worked on their accounts. Since she'd been something of a public relations person for archery she naturally gravitated into doing agency PR work as well.

Denise found that normal life was remarkably easy, almost too easy in fact. She continued to be bothered by a sense that something vital was missing from her life.

"I tried to enjoy myself, and sometimes I did," she said. "But I also felt somewhat lost without the competitions and travel in my life."

Her resumé now included consulting both at home and abroad for Hoyt and Easton. Whenever she had the time she continued to read the archery magazines that still were being delivered to her home. "I'd flip through them to see what was going on, or attend competitions as part of my work with Hoyt or Easton and I gradually found myself becoming interested in who was doing what and where. No (U.S. archer) had really stepped up to take my place, and began thinking I could still be competitive if I tried."

Her brand of 'normal' didn't suit her, not when a major part of her life felt so unfinished, with its one jagged edge scratching at her soul until she finally knew she had to polish it off and be done with it for good.

"I didn't want (my competitive career) to end like it had, with me falling apart, suffering the meltdown and then disappearing," she said. "I decided then that my career wasn't over yet. I'd come back, make another (U.S. Olympic) team and end on a high note, one much different than the last time I'd left it."

Finding the Groove

Denise needed to confide in someone and she had just the person in mind. "I called Tim Strickland and told him I wanted to make another Olympic team," said Denise.

"Do you think I can do this, Tim?" she asked.

"You could," replied Strickland. "You could be better than ever."

"Would you be my coach?" asked Denise.

Strickland thought for a moment before he answered. "Under one condition," he said. "You and I must work together. You can't get input from everybody else in archery. You have to believe in the system that I've put in place, and believe in it totally. If you do that, I'll coach you."

Denise never even hesitated. "Yes," she said.

Coach and archer reunited in 1997. Their common goal: having Denise once more become a member of the U.S. Olympic archery team that would compete in the 2000 Olympics in Australia. To do so, she'd have to qualify as one of the top three shooters at the Olympic Trials scheduled for the spring of 2000.

Denise then quit her job in advertising to take a position as editor of the Salt Lake City-based *Archery Focus,* the bimonthly publication

Me and my mother at the 1999 Pan American Games.

covering Olympic and International competition. She proved her mettle at the magazine many times over, serving not only as editor-in-chief but also as photo, layout and assignment editor as well as ad salesperson. The busy schedule agreed with her and she enjoyed the somewhat different perspective of being an interested and knowledgeable observer on the archery industry's journalistic beat.

She also was able to view her own incomparable experiences in archery from a remove of several years. What an unbelievable trip it had been, she realized. Many people work a lifetime at a passion, sport or intellectual pursuit and yet rarely does anyone receive the remarkable breadth of exposure she'd received, without even expecting it. She simply had been a remarkably gifted archer, one who'd been the right age at the right time and who had been steered in the right directions so that everything meshed to perfection. Such congruence might never occur for any other archer again.

Denise embarked upon her training with renewed determination. With age came wisdom and so no thoughts of relocating to an Olympic training center ever again entered her head. To do so would hinder—not help—as she sought to attain her goal, and so she remained where she felt most comfortable.

Denise, naturally, no longer possessed the level of skill she'd had when she left archery. After such a long layoff from archery she felt stiff and weak the first time she shot. Her mechanics were rusty and she felt awkward using her equipment. She continued to work diligently, however, and gradually regained muscle tone, polished her technique and her shooting soon improved but not to the level she'd been shooting at before she quit. "(The decline) was a humbling experience," she remarked.

Denise remained at *Archery Focus* for a year before moving to Hoyt Archery to write the company's press releases. She soon was promoted to the position of marketing manager. The Hoyt management team knew of Denise's desire to make the Olympic team one last time and wanted to do whatever was feasible to help her attain that goal.

Denise was back on track, and in a good way: *Her* way. "I had a clear sense of what I must do as well as how I must do it," she explained. "I would work while I was in training with Tim. I'd decided that the 2000 Olympics would be it for me, my last shot. I wanted to step up in front of the world, deal with the pressure and leave with my head held high."

Focusing on archery to the exclusion of everything else enjoyable in her life had been a huge mistake. "I needed to feel that my life didn't revolve around archery," said Denise. "I'd take a run

Scott and me after our team won the gold medal in the 1999 Pan American Games.

before work, then take a long lunch so I could shoot for a while. I'd shoot after work too, but I'd never overdo it. Say what you will about 'breathing it and sleeping it,' but it didn't work for me. Balancing my life, as I'd done during the years when I'd been most successful, worked best for me."

Her shooting gradually improved until she once again was shooting at a high level. Denise Parker, it seemed, was finding her groove.

A Return to Competition

What would it be like, Denise sometimes thought, to step back up on the firing line while the entire archery world watched and wondered what would happen next. She pushed those thoughts to the back of her mind. At the first tournament after the self-imposed layoff, her goal was simple: merely show up, not win nor even shoot well.

She returned to competition at the 1998 U.S. National Championships, held in Canton, Michigan, about six months after Denise had re-entered training. Standing on the line in Canton, according to Denise, was the most difficult thing she'd ever done in her life. "When you're scared, the bull's eye looks about the size of a dime."

"I can't begin to explain the pressure I felt," she explained. "It was horrible." She even felt she could read the audience's minds—Will she, Denise, be as good as before? Will she fail? Denise knew her comeback could truly begin only after she'd faced and conquered her demons. She looked beseechingly at Tim, secretly hoping he'd give her the okay to quit. He didn't, of course. And then she started to shoot. With each arrow that cleared the string and sped downfield the pressure lessened. She continued to be aware of everything around her, noticing things that she'd have never noticed when she was 14 and carefree, but which she noticed now. And still the tension flowed from her body. She began to believe that perhaps hers wasn't an impossible dream, and that she would be able to overcome her fears.

"I concentrated on staying totally focused," said Denise. "I'd already attained my goals of showing up and dealing with the pressure of shooting, which were the first steps in what was bound to be a prolonged process."

When Denise later discussed that tournament she dismissed her performance by saying she 'didn't do well.' And yet she finished eighth, a monumental achievement in light of her fragile psychological state at the conclusion of the 1995 Olympic Trials, just three years previously.

Throughout the summer of 1998, Denise shot well enough to be ranked among the nation's top five female archers. As she renewed her mastery of the sport her confidence level increased as well. Her schedule remained the same, although each day she shot only 150 arrows total, or less than half of what she'd shot each day when in training for the 1996 Olympics. Mixed in as well were occasional flights to Indiana where Tim Strickland and his wife, Shirley, now lived.

In 1999, Denise met and started dating Scott Smith. The two soon realized they were falling in love. That summer, Scott occasionally joined Denise at competitions, and she soon grew to rely upon his support and encouragement as much as that of her family and friends during this, her last Olympic odyssey. Scott, who had two young daughters from a previous marriage, was unable to travel to every competition, however, and Denise, for the first time, discovered parting, even briefly, could be extremely difficult.

Denise and Scott that winter found and bought a house together. If she had secretly harbored dreams of competing beyond the 2000 Games, she relinquished them once she and Scott became engaged to be married.

By the end of the winter of '99, Denise was ranked fourth in the U. S. She'd won an individual bronze medal at the 1999 Pan Am Games and a gold medal as part of the U. S. Women's Pan Am team. She'd finished first in the U. S. Nationals, second in the U. S. Open, and third in the U. S. Indoor Championships.

Denise Parker had rediscovered the joy of archery. She'd once fallen in love with archery for the sheer sake of shooting arrows accurately and with near-perfect form and technique, and she now found herself falling in love with those aspects of the sport all over again. She'd briefly lost sight of that joy when it had become darkly shadowed by an all-consuming desire to win. Only after she returned to the sport's basics and found again that sense of joy was she able to glimpse again that which had so thoroughly fascinated her at the beginning. She was fortunate. Many athletes in similar straits find that they've forever lost the magic, and are simply unable or unwilling to venture back to their roots to rediscover what first entranced them about their sports, and compelled them to compete.

The 2000 Olympic Trials

The Trials were to be held in San Diego in the spring of 2000. Qualifying, Denise discovered, would be very different than in the past Trials she'd competed in. Where, in the past, she would step up to the line and shoot her allotted arrows quickly, each in a rhythm as familiar to her as the beating of her heart. This time, however, she would raise the bow, draw the string until the clicker sounded, signaling that the bow was at full draw, and then release the instant the shot felt good, and she would do this over and over for however many arrows must be shot.

It once had been so easy, so natural, and had felt so right.

One arrow at a time. That was how Denise must now approach these Trials, by shooting one arrow at a time.

She began thinking about the magnitude of what she was attempting to do: making the team or not. Her focus became less sharp, for just an instant, but she regained it.

"I hadn't realized how easy it would be to slip back into my old (psychological) ruts," said Denise.

If she must concentrate on shooting a single arrow at a time, then that was what she would do. Denise focused, and shot. Focused and shot. She never allowed herself to slacken her focus. She didn't dare. It would be too easy to do the unimaginable, again.

She remained intensely focused until the last arrow had been shot. Her hand relaxed as the arrow sped downfield and thudded into the target. It was out of her hands. There was nothing more she could do.

Except celebrate. She'd finished in third place and made the 2000 U. S. Olympic Archery Team.

"A tremendous weight seemed to lift from my shoulders," said Denise. "I'd done what had seemed so impossible a few years earlier. "I'd reached my goal." She had prevailed over the toughest competitor of her life—her own psyche.

That September she traveled with the U. S. team to to compete in a test event prior to the Olympics and helped the team to a bronze medal, yet another indication that perhaps the nightmare had ended, at least for now.

Tim and Shirley Strickland along with my Dad in Sydney, Australia.

Training: One Last Time

Denise had made the team. She was 25 now, and mature in every way. That maturity contributed to her ability to enter into training with a fresh outlook on the process, one that included vindicating herself in her own eyes as well as in the eyes of the world.

Soon after she'd made the team Denise spoke with Scott and also her boss at Hoyt. She explained to both of them the need to do her best for her own peace of mind as well as for her teammates and her country. For those reasons, she'd decided to devote between four and five months that summer to training for the Olympics. She would rent a small, unfurnished house in Indiana, close to where Tim Strickland lived, to serve as her home base. The house she later rented, in Milan, Indiana, while adequate in that it kept her sheltered from the elements, could hardly have been called 'homey.' Its only furnishings were a mattress on the floor for sleeping and a small black and white TV for entertainment.

When the time came, Scott helped Denise pack her clothing and gear into their car and then the pair drove back to Indiana together. When Scott flew back to Utah, Denise knew she'd entered upon one of the final legs of her last Olympic journey. She decided to savor the Olympic experience in its entirety, beginning to end. She'd never been able to do so before either because she'd been too young and green, or too consumed by the desire to win.

Denise continued to work with Strickland until it was September, 2000, and nearly time to leave the U. S. for Sidney. She was happy with her shooting even though she had yet to reach the rather astronomic level of accuracy for which she'd once been famous.

The 2000 Olympic Games

This time the U.S. women's archery team was comprised of Denise, Karen Scavotto and Janet Dykman. The men's team was made up of Vic Wunderle, Rod White and Butch Johnson.

Tim Strickland was pleased with the progress Denise had made since she'd been named to the team. "Denise is an accomplished archer, and now she's seasoned," said Strickland. "She's regained her natural style—trusting her subconscious."

When she'd been at her best Denise had been willing to eliminate all conscious thought and let her subconscious take control. "The idea is to let it happen naturally," she'd explained. "That's the Zen of archery."

Olympic Individual Competition

Karen Scavotto was the team's best archer in 2000. Denise knew that of the three women, Karen had the best chance to medal for the U.S.

The individual draw went badly for the U.S., unfortunately, with Karen being matched up against her teammate Denise in the very first round. Knowing that Karen had a better chance than she did to win an individual medal, created an internal conflict for Denise, one she neither needed nor wanted. "I wanted to do my best, and yet I didn't want to knock Karen out," said Denise. "I'd have rather shot against anyone in the competition other than Karen."

Karen Scavotto won the shoot-off and moved on to finish eighth overall in the individual competition.

Olympic Team Competition

The U.S. women's team shot well enough to qualify for the quarter-finals. Their combined score had been very good, and the women hoped to maintain their momentum. They might have done so, too, had they not immediately been matched with the Koreans, who hadn't lost a head-to-head competition since the 1970s. Should the Americans prevail against the Koreans they would have proceeded to the semifinals, or top four teams.

"We felt sure we could beat anyone except the Koreans," recalled Denise.

The U.S. women again shot a superb score—the second highest

score of the entire competition. The first highest? Shot by the Koreans when they knocked the U.S. team out of medal contention.

The U.S. women's archery team finished in fifth place, a great showing, and yet the teammates knew had they faced any team other than the Koreans in the second round they would have qualified for the medal round. The luck of the draw, which in this case was all bad, had conspired to send the suddenly hot-shooting U. S. women's team home without a medal. Any other draw result and the women very easily might have been wearing silver or bronze.

Karen and me practicing prior to our competition at the 2000 Olympic Games in Sydney, Australia.

Saying Good-bye

Denise left Sydney having done what she set out to do. She at last felt satisfied with her life and her career. She'd gone out gracefully, with her head held high, and very nearly with yet another Olympic medal for her yeoman-efforts in Sydney.

"I could look back now with no regrets," said Denise. "I was ready to move on to live the rest of my life."

Denise Parker knows she's been blessed with talent and opportunities that other people never get or never even attempt to develop. She's won every meaningful U. S. archery competition as well as

Denise Parker

Here is a picture of me competing which was broadcast on the jumbo tron at the 2000 Olympics in Sydney.

having won many gold medals at the most important competitions of the Western Hemisphere, the Pan Am Games. She's won an Olympic medal and been a member of three Olympic teams over a span of 12 years.

"I don't feel like I'm more successful because I won a bronze medal," said Denise. "Nor am I less successful because I failed to win gold. It's impossible for every person competing at the Olympics to win gold. In that way, the Olympics parallels life. Not everyone will win the gold. Life isn't always up, up and up. You'll have downs, too. Doing your best, regardless of ups and downs, is what matters most when all is said and done." ∎

Chapter 13

Life: So Much More!

Heart, Hearth and Home

Denise and Scott were married not long after she returned to the U. S. from Sydney. The pair settled down in the home they'd purchased together and where on many weekends they were joined by Scott's two daughters Madeline and McCayla who, since the marriage, had become Denise's new step-daughters.

The Smiths welcomed Jake in July 2003, and Nicklaus in September 2005. Jake was named after Bob "Jake" Jacobson, one of Denise's early archery instructors. The name Nicklaus reflects a love of golf and The Golden Bear, Jack Nicklaus, on behalf of both husband and wife. Denise, as might be expected, is an outstanding golfer which is a good thing since golf is Scott's primary passion, after his family, of course.

Me and my two step-daughters, Madeline and McCayla, my husband Scott and our sons Jake and Nicklaus.

I enjoy playing golf as one of my activities during my free time.

So Much More!

Denise no longer is the starry-eyed 14-year-old with a gift so special it wasn't too far-fetched to imagine that perhaps she had been blessed by Artemis, the Greek goddess of the hunt. Artemis—called 'Diana' by the Romans—hunted with bow and arrow. The Greeks believed her home was on Mount Olympus, the place that gave the Olympic Games their name, and from which she'd descend on occasion to help some mortal out of the jam into which he or she had become ensnared.

Today she is a grown woman, a mother and wife, and a well-respected executive who just happened to have an extraordinary talent for archery. She still dreams like the Denise of 1988, only those dreams now center on her children.

"The dreams I'd like to pursue are all about my kids," said Denise. "I'd like them to shoot archery and learn to enjoy it as a sport but more importantly, I just want them to find their own passions. I want to do lots of things with them, the way I was able to have fun with my parents no matter what they decided to do."

Like most parents, Denise wonders how her own children will someday grade her as a parent. "I can't help but wonder, if Nick or Jake are successful, if I'll be there to love and encourage them, no matter what. I'd like to think I would, and yet I don't think any parent really knows how he or she will react until the time is actually upon them."

Denise, understandably considering her competitiveness, worries that should that time come, when one or both of her children exhibit tremendous talent of some sort, will she forget her own experiences and become overbearing or too demanding?

No one can see into the future, of course. But Denise has a definite advantage in that she can still see rather vividly into the window on her past to a time when one teenager wanted nothing more than a father and her parents unconditional love.

"I know one thing," said Denise, in conclusion. "I never want my children to think that the amount of love I have for them will ever be dependent on their success" (whether in school, sports, music or) "in any other activity."

Denise Parker has always known what she wants. And once she knows it, she pursues it with every ounce of energy and resolve in her being.

One can't help but feel that Denise's children are among the world's luckiest. They have a mother who's been there, done that, and is wise enough to have benefited from her many experiences. And in the Olympics of life, a gold medal mother trumps a gold medal archer every time! ■

SAVE OUR HERITAGE

"Your investment in the future of archery and bowhunting!"

With the purchase of this book you are supporting programs that help to grow the sports you love so much—archery and bowhunting. SOH book proceeds support an initiative dubbed "Community Archery Programs" or CAP. This program attempts to make archery and bowhunting as convenient and accessible to as many people as possible within a community. Without repeated exposures and easy access to archery shooting facilities and bowhunting opportunities in their local area we are in jeopardy of losing future generations of archers and bowhunters. To find out more about our programs please visit www.archerytrade.org.

ATA Grant Funding for School Archery Programs

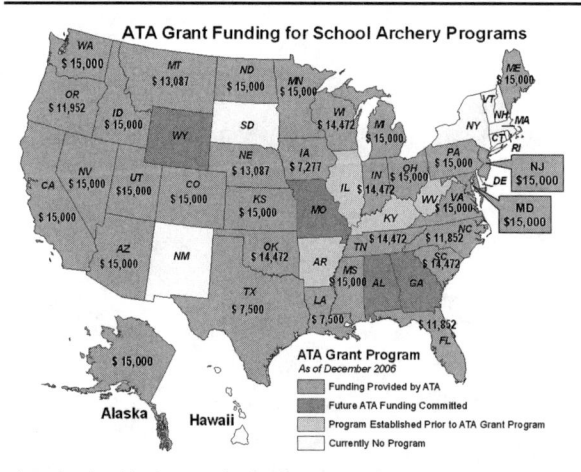

ATA Grant Program
As of December 2006

- Funding Provided by ATA
- Future ATA Funding Committed
- Program Established Prior to ATA Grant Program
- Currently No Program

The CAP strategy is to begin with clusters of schools as a starting point and then expand to after-school and public and nonprofit recreational programs surrounding these schools. ATA implemented a School Archery Program Initiation Grant program between 2004 and 2007. ATA plans to use SOH funding to provide additional grants in the future for CAP program priorities.

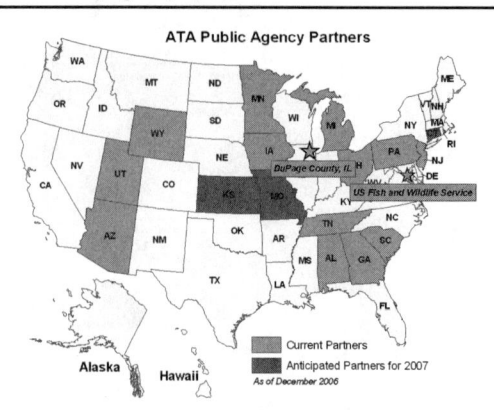

ATA Public Agency Partners

- Current Partners
- Anticipated Partners for 2007

As of December 2006

Another CAP strategy is to capitalize on existing relationships, and not waste time or money reinventing agency, governmental, or any other organization's existing programs. CAP programs are developed through formal partnerships with federal, state, and county agencies. Investing in public agency programs and working to secure public funds and resources will insure the longevity of the programs.

LOOKING FOR AN ARCHERY RETAILER?

ARCHERYSEARCH◉COM

LOOKING FOR AN ARCHERY INSTRUCTOR?

ARCHERYSEARCH◉COM

LOOKING FOR AN ARCHERY RANGE?

ARCHERYSEARCH◉COM

LOOKING FOR AN ARCHERY CLUB?

ARCHERYSEARCH◉COM

Where you'll find all the answers to your archery and bowhunting questions

WOODS N' WATER PRESS

Other titles available from the Save Our Heritage book program include:

Fail-Proof Tactics for Whitetail Bowhunting
Bob McNally
208 pages, 140+ photos, color insert, Hardcover
$24.95

The Bowhunter's Field Manual
Judd Cooney
208 pages, 80+ photos, color insert, Hardcover
$24.95

The Complete Bowhunting Journal
Rick Sapp
208 pages, 100+ photos, color insert, Hardcover
$24.95

Bowhunting Forests & Deep Woods
Greg Miller
240 pages, 100+ photos, Hardcover $24.95

Bowhunting's Superbucks
Kathy Etling
240 pages, 80+ photos, color insert, Hardcover
$24.95

Bowhunting Tactics That Deliver Trophies
Steve Bartylla
208 pages, 80+ photos, color insert, Hardcover
$24.95

Ask for these exciting and informative titles at your local sporting goods dealer or order on-line at www.atabooks.com. Call our office at 1-800-652-7527 or write to us at Woods N' Water Press, P.O. Box 550, Florida, NY 10921 for a catalog. We thank you for your support!